THE CLIENT MAGNET METHOD

HOW TO STOP CHASING GIGS, ATTRACT HIGH-PAYING CLIENTS, AND BUILD A THRIVING BUSINESS YOU LOVE

MIKE GLEN ROY

The Client Magnet Method for Creative Freelancers

Publisher: Mike Glen Roy, LLC. And Creative Freelance Revolution.

Print Edition ISBN:
978-1-944943-02-8
Print Edition ISBN-13:
1-944943-02-1

Ebook Edition ISBN:
978-1-944943-03-5
Ebook Edition ISBN-13:
1-944943-03-X

Printed in the United States of America.
First Edition: March 2026.

For Mom and Dad. Even when I doubted by abilities, you never did. My creative journey would have been much harder without having you in my corner every step of the way. Thank you for your loving support.

CONTENTS

THE CLIENT MAGNET METHOD FOR CREATIVE FREELANCERS

Unlock the Secrets to Attracting and Retaining High-Value Dream Clients

Unleash the power of the *Client Magnet Method*, a game-changing approach that will revolutionize your ability to consistently attract your ideal clients and build a thriving freelance business. Inside this guide, you'll discover a treasure trove of actionable strategies, relationship-building techniques, and insider tips for client retention. Armed with these invaluable insights, you'll be equipped to effectively communicate, deeply understand client needs, and forge long-term partnerships that fuel your success. Get ready to unlock the full potential of your freelance career and magnetize high-paying dream clients who truly recognize and value your worth.

HOW TO ACCESS YOUR BOOK BONUSES

This super-useful book you hold in your hands is just *part* of the fun. I have more in store for you!

I've created a selection of special downloadable bonuses just for you, dear reader. You can find them here:

TheClientMagnetMethod.com

I know you might want to hop over there now and see what goodies are waiting for you. If you do, be sure to jump back into the book so you can learn how to use them to help you get great clients.

FOREWORD

The best way to upgrade a freelance career is to get better clients. They challenge you, pay you more and talk about you more. And you don't get better clients by working hard for lousy clients. You get better clients by becoming the kind of freelancer that better clients want to hire.

– Seth Godin

Stop! Read This First.

Dear Reader,

I feel compelled in this age where we're awash with information to do you a favor: I'd like to go ahead and state what to expect in the following pages, should you decide it's worth your time to keep reading. If you decide this is not worth reading, then I've just saved you a few hours of your valuable time. You're welcome!

What's This Book About?

This book is for people who are in a creative field such as graphic design, video editing, writing, or photography, and they want to either start their own freelance business or improve their existing one. It walks you through different ways on how to attract and win clients who are willing to pay you for your creative services.

Who The Heck Are You?

I'm just a fellow creative professional, just like you, who managed to work through my own personal challenges and build an amazing freelance business that's changed my life. This business allows me to work from home, whenever I want to, and it pays more than enough to not just cover my bills, but also to have fun vacations and store up a nest-egg should I decide I don't feel like freelancing anymore. (A point that I haven't come to yet at the time of this writing… which is fine, I'm still having way too much fun in the journey anyway.)

Why Did You Write It?

I wrote this for several reasons… the first one is that I really enjoy helping people, and one of the best ways that I think there is to help people is to "teach them to fish"… to enable and empower them to hone their gifts, talents, and skills to improve their lives.

I also wrote this because I not only love helping people, but I also am seeing a revolution taking place and it sounded like fun to be a part of it. The revolution I'm referring to is what I call the Creative Freelance Revolution, and in the grand scheme of things, it's really just starting… so welcome to the party!

If you're interested more about this revolution, you can read more at creativefreelancerevolution.com, where I talk about all kinds of things related to building your creative freelancing business, including mindsets that are useful to us as freelancers, industry trends that shape the forces that we work in, and other relevant topics.

Never Mind That... Just Show Me The Money!

Maybe you aren't concerned with revolutions, however nonviolent they may be. Maybe you just want to be able to do something as quickly as possible to pay the bills that isn't digging ditches or sitting in a cubicle in an air-conditioned office somewhere… and that's totally okay, too. In fact, that's exactly what this book is designed for: to give you the quickest, most no-nonsense (but most effective) way to build your creative freelance business by filling your calendar with great clients who appreciate your talents - and who are happy to pay you for them.

To that end, I want to give you a promise… and I'd like a promise from you in return.

The promise I give you is that I won't waste your time with a lot of fluff and filler. For example, I'm not going to go into detail, textbook-style, about all the ins and outs of every single platform you can possibly use to get clients. Instead, I'll make you aware of what's out there as of the writing of this book, and then single out the BEST ONE that's actually worked for me, and tell you more about it.

Along with that, I also promise you that the stuff I've written in this book isn't me doing an internet search for ways to get clients, or using an A.I. to write it, and then regurgitating it back out on the page. Rather, the things I'll be showing you are REAL WAYS that I've gotten actual, paying clients for my OWN freelance business.

Here's the catch, and it's the promise that I'd like from you should you decide to keep reading: **that you will make a sincere effort to not only learn what you read in these pages, but to also put them into practice… and to not give up until you achieve your first bit of success in the form of a great client.**

That "gateway client" is life-changing in and of themselves… because now the dream is real, you wake up to the fact that you CAN actually get paid to do this! You realize that all the work and effort really does pay off. That oozy, nagging voice in the back of your mind that's been saying *"nobody's gonna actually pay you to do what you love, you know that, right?"* just got a little quieter. And now you can go and get some more great clients… with even *more* confidence. The snowball effect has begun!

Now, my assumption is that you're good at what you do, and you can provide a valuable creative service. Compared to all the hard work you've done and all the long hours you've spent to get to this point in your career, I'm willing to bet that putting some of the things I'll be showing you into place will be much easier. Chances are, you've already done some of them, and so you're not starting from scratch… and that's even better.

No matter where you are in your journey, I want you to keep in mind this very important phrase that one of my mentors gave me: **"Success Is Inevitable"**. And it is… when we show up consistently and do the work, the results we're looking for ***will*** happen.

Before You Go... Take This

There's one more thing that I'd like to offer you before we begin. It will come in handy during the inevitable times when you come across a challenge or obstacle that seems too difficult. Or, when you just feel discouraged at any point your journey to become the freelancer you want to be.

That thing I'd like to give you is an email to my personal inbox… ***mike@creativefreelancerevolution.com.*** Drop me a line anytime. While I can't guarantee I'll be able to get to you right away, I do make it a priority to read and respond to each and every email that I get from my fellow freelancers.

And now, without further ado…

… let's become **magnetic!**

INTRO TO THE CLIENT MAGNET METHOD

Greetings, Superstar Creative Freelancer!

(Also, hello to those of you who *aspire* to be superstar creative freelancers… this is for you as well!)

You're reading this right now because somehow you came across my little corner o' the internet and you found this resource. Perhaps you figure it's worth a few minutes to spend reading it, that it might help you get more clients for your freelancing business. In any case, you're spending time investing in yourself, and I want you to know that I respect the heck out of you for it.

The fact that we're occupying this same brain-space at this moment is, to me, nothing short of miraculous… and I thank you for letting me into your world. In exchange for your time and attention, I promise that I will not hold back… I'll share **everything** I know about the single most important thing that helped me build a six-figure solo creative freelance business.

If my plan of world domination comes to fruition, then I will develop workshops, courses, masterminds, and stuff like that, and charge a lot more than what you paid for this book. But, here's a lil' secret just between friends: the most important stuff you'd learn in those will be right here, amongst these very pages.

The reason I wrote this book is because I wanted to discover and address the **number one concern** that my fellow freelancers have in building up their business. It wasn't hard to find, because that concern is pretty much **unanimous**. It revolves around **one** theme:

> ***"How do I get great clients?"***

It's understandable that this would be our number one-rated concern as independent creative business owners. Getting clients isn't something many of us have the **background** for, because many of us didn't go to school to learn how to do it.

Or, maybe all this "business-y" talk just feels really weird because you never saw yourself as a "business owner"... it feels too much like something your dad would do. I totally get it. If it *does* feel too weird, just substitute "business" for *"the creative thing you do that you'd actually like to get paid for."* (Sure, it's wordy, but it works.)

Perhaps you're just **beginning** your freelancing journey, and you figure learning how to get clients is a good way to start. Kudos to you... it **is**! As you'll soon learn, all it takes to give a freelance career a good start is ONE great client.

Or, maybe you're a **seasoned** freelancer who's tired of the never-ending rat race of hunting down people willing to pay you to do what you love to do for a living. OR... maybe you don't love it quite so much any more… you're burned out and just about ready to throw in the towel, and you're considering taking up Uncle Augie's offer to work his food truck. (At least you know good ol' Augie will pay on time!)

Whomever you are, and wherever you are in your quest to become a self-sufficient creative professional, **this book is for you.**

Why I Can Help You Get Clients (And Build Your Freelance Business)

While I haven't *always* had a successful creative freelance business, I have one now. It's been quite a journey… but it's been worth it.

When I first went freelance years ago, I had just graduated from college with an art degree. I even had a piece of paper called a diploma that said so! But while I felt prepared to do a variety of creative tasks, I was WAY unprepared for a creative career as a freelancer. Getting clients was one of the MANY struggles I dealt with at that time. Besides a lack of **knowledge** of how to actually get clients, I also dealt with a host of bad habits, negative mindsets, and ignorance about how to run an actual business. (To be fair, this is because at that time I actually didn't consider it to be a business!)

After flailing around awhile as a newly minted freelancer, I got bailed out of having to do the solo business thing by getting a creative job as an employee. I got another job after that, a "dream job" at an aspiring creative studio working on commercials and film projects. I was the seventeenth person hired there, and within years I had helped that studio grow to over 500 people and branches in several different cities.

I got to develop my creative skills on a ton of different projects. I also got to learn how to conduct meetings with clients, how to work directly in front of them, how to pitch work to them, and even how to deal with them in difficult situations. I learned about the financials of a job, how it all breaks down, and who gets a piece of the "pie" of an overall creative budget. I also learned what it was like on the "other side" of the client / freelancer equation… how companies staff creative roles, the kind of people they look for, and how they decide to hire them. It was an amazing journey, and I will always be grateful for the projects, the experience, and the people that helped me develop into the professional that I am today.

Alas, as many of us can remember, years into my career a little thing called COVID-19 happened. My studio ended up letting go of everyone in the commercial division, my professional home for over twenty-one years. I was faced with two choices: I could either try to get hired on at another company… OR I could take a leap and do something that I had been wanting to do for years: hang out my own shingle and **go freelance**.

I chose freelancing. (And I'm so glad that I did!)

This time, freelancing was very different. I wasn't the same freshly graduated newbie that I was years ago. I had a body of work, I had professional authority, and I knew how to deal with clients. I found out that finding them, relating to them, and even negotiating with them about "scary topics" like pay rates wasn't very difficult once I learned how. What I didn't yet know how to do, I found out how to do … because I was *determined* to make my freelancing business work.

Now, after growing my freelance business to over six figures per year, I'm as satisfied with my career as I've ever been. I've been able to spend more time with my family, to engage in new hobbies and activities, and to contribute to causes that I believe in. I also feel much more secure and confident about my future than I ever have before.

I also really like the feeling that I'm in the middle of a sort of revolution… what I call the creative freelance revolution… where all kinds of indie creatives are discovering that they can build their own business that supports their lifestyle and their loved ones by doing what they enjoy doing. Best of all, we can do this from the comfort of our home office, or from a beach on Waikiki, or anywhere in between (provided the internet connection is good enough!)

At the same time, I've always gotten a big kick out of teaching and coaching people. I found that I really enjoyed helping a few of my peers who had recently been let go of their company. I liked talking to them about their goals and their struggles, and helping them get on their feet and do something they really wanted to do. I enjoyed that feeling of contribution. It fulfilled me in a way that the usual creative projects didn't, because I felt like I actually improved someone's quality of life.

That's why I started a purposeful business focused on teaching and coaching my fellow creatives just like you, to share what I've learned along the way to building my own business.

My journey won't be the exact same as yours… but there *will* be many similarities. My stories are echoes of your stories, and my struggles are like your struggles. I know this because I was once where you might be now… wondering if it gets better from here. (I can tell you with conviction that it *does,* when you put in the effort to make it better.) I also wondered if there were people out there that I could learn from, who understood exactly what I was going through and who could help me find the next few steps. (Spoiler alert: there *are*.)

It's not always going to be easy. Things as rewarding as this are rarely easy. Getting started is the hardest part. Taking the next step is the second hardest. But as your business grows, and you put these things into place that I'm about to teach you, it *does* get easier as you go along… and as you build your confidence, your accomplishments, and your list of high-quality clients.

I can also tell you that the end results are worth it. They're absolutely life-changing, in the most positive way possible.

So… without further ado… let's begin!

Why Getting Clients Is Important

I'm sure you already know that clients are *important* to your creative freelance business. (*"Duh, Mike… that's why I'm even reading this!"*)

I think that it helps in the beginning to clarify WHY our client-getting goals are so important, and why they can help us. It gets us excited about the possibilities, and it energizes us by helping us visualize our future success.

So here are some very real (and very powerful) reasons why clients are so important to our freelancing:

- Clients pay us **money**, which is the **lifeblood** of our business. Without blood, there's no life, and our business dies.
- As freelancers, it's critical for our business to **succeed**. If we don't have a thriving business, we don't get to live the life we want, for us *or* our loved ones. It means we have to go get a job as an employee and most likely give up our freedoms and the other great things we enjoy as freelancers. (A hearty "NO THANKS" to that!)
- Clients are so significant that even if everything *else* in our business is mediocre, we can still have a business as long as there are clients. For example, you might be unorganized, bad at keeping records, and slow to send out invoices. You might even be in the middle of the pack talent-wise. But if you have clients, your business will still live. (We definitely want to work on those other things, by the way… so we can ensure the clients that you DO have actually *stay* your clients!)
- When we have clients who pay us what we're worth, and who you enjoy working with us, it unlocks the possibility for the *rest* of our business to thrive. Simply put, good clients just makes every thing else about our business *easier*. (Which is good news for many of us "reluctant" business owners… because we need all the help we can get!)
- An "easy" business means we spend **less** time doing the things we **don't want** to do, like prowl around the internet for potential clients. I can guarantee that you will enjoy freelancing (and life in general) much more when you spend *less* time doing the stuff you *don't* want to do… and MORE time doing the stuff you

actually *like* doing. (Now doesn't that sound like a reason to get up in the morning?)

"But... Why Is It So Hard To Get Clients?"

It's actually not that difficult to get clients... you can go on Upwork or some other freelancing "meat markets" like it, offer your services for pennies on the dollar, and get clients. You can also call around to your friends or family and ask them if they need anything done, and not to worry about paying you. You'll get clients. (Usually just not the "right" KIND of clients... that's a whole other story.)

The "right" kind of clients are more difficult to get. The "right" kind of clients are the ones who pay you what you're worth. They're also easy to work with because they're professional, kind, polite, and respectful. Finally, they actually pay you WHEN they say they will pay you, and they don't have to be constantly reminded to do so.

Yes, these people *do* exist! They're not unicorns or gnomes or any other storybook creature who only live in fairy tales. They're **real people**, just like you and me. They have **budgets** to hire capable freelancers, they have **projects** they need done, and they need someone just like YOU do help them.

As a solo freelancer, we are the single point of failure in our business. We might have all the talent in the world, **but if we don't have the skills required to get and retain clients, then that talent is not being put to use.**

Getting clients IS a skill, just like typography or videography or writing a proper article. It's a skill **anyone** can learn. And what do we do when we lack a skill? We put our thinking caps on, we grab a pencil and tablet, and we get to work **acquiring** that skill!

Don't feel bad about yourself if you feel lacking in the skill of getting clients. Maybe you never felt the need to focus on it before. They usually don't teach things like sales or pitching or getting clients in universities, film schools, or your local art institute… so maybe you never had the opportunity to learn it. **The important thing** is, you're here now, and you've found in your hands the "secret sauce" to getting clients like clockwork… whenever you need them… without wasting a bunch of time or doing stuff you hate doing.

The truth is, *everybody* in the business world is scrambling right now to figure out how to sell people products and services and how to get clients. That's because it's not as easy as it used to be… because the client-getting game has *changed,* for a number of reasons we'll talk about next.

WHY THE "GAME" HAS CHANGED

In recent years, there have existed a number of factors that have made it more difficult to get clients - and customers - than it *used* to be. In fact, these same factors have made it harder to relate to each other as humans in general! It stands to reason that these same things would affect the way we do business with each other on a daily basis.

A Lack Of Trust

For one thing, there's been a **decrease in trust**. There's an overall lack of trust in our neighbor, a lack of trust in institutions, and a lack of trust in people who claim to have authority. Gone are the days when we read every single email or answered every single call. Now, we build up our walls out of necessity. And for good reason: barbarian hordes are out there, and they're after blood!

Groundbreaking technologies like Artificial Intelligence have been a double-edged sword: while they've done a lot of positive things, they've also enabled more scams, fraud, and digital tomfoolery in general. From the calls we get, to the videos we see online, to the heads that talk on our tv's, we can no longer afford to blindly trust people like we might have in the past.

Since we're all in the same boat, this decrease in trust goes for your potential clients as well. In this book we'll discuss techniques to break down those trust barriers so that you will be a beacon of trustworthiness to them, and enjoy life within their "**circle of trust.**" (*"...and you want to be in the Circle Of Trust, don't you, Greg?" He says in his best Robert De Niro voice.*)

"Chasing" Is Creepy

Due to that same trust issue, the strategy of "chasing" or "spamming" clients is also becoming less and less effective. While you may have heard this being recommended as a strategy, it's not one that I recommend in this book. Not only does it feel weird, aggressive, and inauthentic, **it also doesn't work very well.**

Have you heard about (or remember) the old days when door-to-door salespeople roamed residential neighborhoods? In those days, you might let some random guy in your house, and stand there and watch as he poured dirt on your carpet so he could demonstrate how his vacuum thingy worked. These days, that same guy gets a restraining order slapped on him... or a fist to the windpipe!

We instinctively mistrust the person who chases us down, stuffs our inbox full of messages, or calls us repeatedly. Is it any wonder that *your* clients aren't responding, either? We'll talk later on about "creep-free" ways to genuinely connect with your clients that are much more effective.

Too Many Options (And Too Much Noise)

We have more **options** than ever before in every aspect of our lives, from the food we eat to the people we associate with. Instead of having a *few* options of freelancers to hire from, our clients have *hundreds* or even *thousands*.

But while options have increased, the "noise" has increased as well. If you're an audio-based freelancer, you know very well the term "signal to noise ratio"... and while you have tools that can separate the signal from the noise in an audio file, it's a bit harder to do that in real life with all the options we have available. With the tips in this guide, you'll be able to **cut through the clutter** and offer a clear value proposition to your clients so they can see you are the real deal as quickly and effectively as possible.

Lack Of Attention

Due to all the options and noise, we modern-day humans all suffer to some degree from a **lack of attention.** Our clients' attention spans have **decreased substantially,** making it difficult to stand out to them. It's also challenging to retain people's attention long enough to facilitate meaningful contact. Your clients' lives are busy and fragmented, and it's a good idea to respect every minute of time that they're able to spend with you.

We all possess a bundle of neurons in our brains called the **Reticular Activating System**. Its job is to filter out information, letting through the important info while disregarding the rest. As you can imagine, the average person's Reticular Activating System is red-lining just about all of the time, working hard to filter out all that noise!

Your clients are no different. We will learn how to get past their R.A.S., and stand out from all the muck and noise. Then you'll be on your way to becoming a valued and trusted part of their business.

The "Rise Of The Robots"

I'd be telling a fib if I didn't say that the rapid onset of Artificial Intelligence hasn't affected all of us job-seekers in a profound way. It seems like A.I. and Machine Learning have infiltrated every aspect of the work people do… and that even includes creative work. So, how in the world do we become magnetic when our clients seem to want to run into the cold, metallic embrace of the machines that promise cheap (or free) labor?

I had this very thing in mind when I crafted this resource. As a result, every strategy I give you, from becoming very good at what you do, to establishing authority, and even to being charismatic, allow you to be something that the machines aren't, and never will be: an **authentic, creatively minded human being** who has REAL solutions and who is a pleasure to work with. These are qualities that your **ideal** clients (who we will also talk about) are looking for… and they'll find them in *you*.

Learn The Game, And You Can Master It.

All of these things seem to have made doing business more challenging, and they have certainly made our lives as freelancers looking to get great clients and great work tough as well. The silver lining is that once we've gotten through the barriers and done great work with a client, and when they've seen we can be relied upon, then we're "**in**"!

It's essential to realize that just as it's hard for us to get great clients, it's also hard for *them* to find great *freelancers*. When they realize you're a keeper, and as you progress in your professional relationship with them, they will value you and keep you at the top of their list... and gladly compensate you what your expertise is worth.

HOW IS THIS "METHOD" DIFFERENT?

"I've been trying to get clients and nothing has worked. How is this 'method' any different?"

One reason why you haven't found clients (or enough of them) could be because you're **not looking in the right place.** They may not hang out in the platforms or forums online that *you* do.

For example, you might feel the need to post on a social platform where everybody seems to be, such as Facebook or Instagram or Twitter (Or X or whatever they're calling themselves these days.) Every time you post, you might get a lot of kudos from Aunt Edna who spends most of her free hours on the platform. She really likes how you "draw" things (you gave up long ago trying to explain to Aunt Edna that you don't actually "draw" the pictures, you "render" them). Maybe this feels affirming… after all, when nobody else responds, at least you know Edna will. But the question is, does that really get you paying clients?

Another example is, you might feel the need to post where you see other creatives posting *their* work, people you admire and want to be like. That seems right, doesn't it? You happen to be scrolling through Instagram and you see someone putting up really cool character animations. It stands to reason that's where YOU should put up yours too right? **Not necessarily.** There might be a lot of eyeballs looking at it and even commenting on it, but it might not be the eyeballs with projects and money to pay you. This might also take you down the wrong rabbit hole of trying to please your peers, distracting you from your *real* mission of getting clients.

This last one is what I call the "**shop talk fallacy**". It's the idea that you go where you see work being shown and commented on by other people doing the same kind of work. Then you spend time putting your work there, reading comments from others who do the same work, and you comment on their work. It becomes a kind of echo chamber, or in best cases, a support group of sorts… you feel like you're getting *something* out of it, because there's a lot of interaction and sharing going on, and you certainly spend a lot of time there… but the question is… **are you actually getting client leads** from those interactions? Are people contacting you with **paying jobs**?

Another possible reason you haven't found the right clients could be that you simply aren't looking for them the right way, or doing anything to get them. Maybe you feel that if your work alone is good enough, and you want it bad enough, then the universe will align itself to give you what you want. If this is you, then I hate to be the one to tell you this, but… **you're living in a dream**. Pinch yourself, go fail a few times, do whatever you need to do to wake yourself up. Go ahead, I'll wait. It's okay, I'll still be here when you get back.

Or, maybe you *have* done a lot of things to get clients, and tried really hard… it just hasn't resulted in the ideal clients you really want. Not nearly enough to pay the bills.

Maybe it's been "feast or famine"… you've gotten a great gig here and there, but it's not consistent enough to generate a reliable income, much less grow a business. You KNOW what you do has value, but you're really frustrated and ready to give up.

It could be you're much closer than you think you are.

It could be…

… that you just haven't discovered how to make yourself …

… MAGNETIC.

WHAT IT MEANS TO BE MAGNETIC

IN YOUR CREATIVE FREELANCE BUSINESS

Being *magnetic* means....

- You can stop CHASING after clients... instead, they come chasing after YOU.
- You've ALIGNED yourself with the NEEDS of your client. They have a project and they have a high degree of certainty that YOU are the person who can help them with it.
- You've developed the COMPETENCE to fulfill a creative need with skill, speed, and professionalism.
- You've attained the AUTHORITY to show that you can fulfill that need with well-crafted marketing materials and other things that show that you're someone who can accomplish a creative goal for a client.
- You've claimed a specific POSITION within the marketplace that is definable and valuable... and one where you can thrive.
- You've positioned yourself on the right PLATFORMS to be seen where your ideal clients are.

- You've connected with a prospective client at the right TIME when they need someone just like you to help them.
- You've attained a level of CHARISMA that makes clients feel they *want* to work with you, because they *enjoy* working with you.
- You're on your way to building a NETWORK of evangelists and referral partners who work behind the scenes to bring you clients on a silver platter.
- Finally… (and, I think this is the BEST part!)… you can spend less time doing the stuff you don't like doing, and more time doing stuff you *want* to do.

The Problem With "Selling Yourself"

Let me make something very clear: when I talk about getting clients, I'm making an important distinction between the traditional idea of "sales" and what I *actually* do (and **teach** how to do) to get clients.

The word "**sales**" has gotten itself a bad rap. It's a word that conjures up images of slick, sly hucksters that saunter up to you and can't wait to separate you from your hard-earned cash. (In fact, I purposely try to steer clear of actually using the word "sales" or "selling" in any of this… precisely because of this connotation!)

I've always been terrible at sales. I remember as a kid trying to sell magazines for my school to raise funds for something or other. There I was, a nervous little guy, standing on someone's front porch, ringing their doorbell with trembling hands, and hoping that nobody would answer. When they actually did, I reluctantly held out my order form to them: *"Uh... hi. You wanna buy some magazines?"* Needless to say, I didn't sell very many magazines in my very short sales career. And since I hated doing it, I didn't do it for very long... I think I made it about three houses down the block before giving up. (To make matters even worse, once I got home, I tried selling a magazine to my mom... and I even struck out there, too! Cmon', mom, give a guy a break!)

Many of us creatives steer way clear of the idea of sales... we'd do just about **anything** to avoid being seen as "slimy" or "sleazy". Or maybe we see it as crossing over into a place where we don't feel authentic.

Ok, I think you get the idea... for most of us creative-types, sales sucks, and we don't really want to do it. So I have some good news and I have some bad news.

First, the bad news: if you want to be a successful creative person, you're gonna have to (gulp) SELL yourself in some fashion. There, I said it. Go ahead, throw your tantrum, go outside and scream and shake your little fist at the sky, and then come back for the good news.

Here's the good news: **it's not as bad as you might think.**

Sure, there are people out there who advocate for creative freelancers to engage in the more "traditional" idea of sales: get the contact info for a lot of people, spam them with requests, and ask them if they would like to hire them for a job. It's a "numbers game": if pretty much any of us just "buckle down" and contact a hundred people, then a few of them will end up as clients.

I'm not gonna say this strategy won't work, because it actually ***does***. The robocalls we get from on our phones from call centers every day are a testament to that.

Now, there is another way, an alternative to using the "brute force" method of chasing after clients: and that way is what I call the **Client Magnet Method**.

This is when you put the things in place to attract clients who come to YOU when they want to hire you. And they're not just any clients… they're *quality* clients, who value you and pay you what you're worth.

That's right… no cold-calling, cold-emailing, or trying over and over to convince complete strangers of your value… these clients contact YOU for work.

Now, doesn't that sound much more fun?

How I Developed The Client Magnet Method

Maybe at this point you're saying something along the lines of this:

"OK, OK… I Get It. I'm Ready To Hear About This Method! Part of me wants to not believe you… but I want to believe so bad that I'm going to keep reading."

This method is simply a set of steps you can take…. a checklist, if you will… and at the end of those steps, you get your ideal clients, over and over, on repeat.

It's kind of like the recipe for a cake. You follow the recipe, and voila, you eventually get a delicious cake. (If you like cake, that is… I don't really like cake, but most people do, and so that's why I use cake as an example, but I digress.)

As I mentioned earlier, I started freelancing many moons ago, as a green artist fresh out of university. I did NOT do very many of these steps that I'm about to show you, because I didn't *know* to do them. I fumbled around and actually threw obstacles in front of myself. (It's almost as if I didn't WANT to get clients… and… well, that's a whole other story I'll tell you later.)

Anyway, fast forward to years later, and I was an accomplished artist in my field… but I'd just lost my job. (Thanks, Covid!) I had always wanted to get back into the freelance world, so I thought, now is my chance. I had a family to support. I had ZERO interest in changing careers to some other vocation that I hadn't prepared for. (I would feel like I had wasted twenty-plus years of my life, and I was definitely not interested in that!)

So, more determined than ever, I decided to get out of my comfort zone and do whatever it took to get the clients that I needed to work from home and leverage the skills that I had spent all that time developing.

I took the experience I had gained in my creative field, and added to that what I had learned from various ventures such as marketing and pitching. I combined all that into a focused effort to get the exact clients I wanted, to support the lifestyle for my family and I that I desired to have.

And… it *worked*.

The clients showed up. They brought work. They brought money, which was nice when it came time to do things like pay for vacations and support my family's Starbucks habit.

At times, there were so many clients that I had to turn them away. It felt strange to do so, but it was an awesome problem to have, if you can even *call* it a problem.

On my journey I encountered others who hadn't quite experienced the same level of success that I had. And to be honest, many of them seemed to have even more talent and experience than I had possessed, and even worked harder and longer hours, **but they still seemed to have trouble getting clients.**

This fascinated me, and I became determined to find out more.

I sat down and pulled apart what I had done to get these great clients that had helped grow my business. What was so different about my early freelancing experience (which was terrible) and now (which was awesome)? What were the parts and pieces of this success? Was it a flash in the pan, or were there repeatable, definable elements to it that I could teach to someone else… so that they, too, could have the level of success getting clients that I had?

So I did some research. I dug through my business, my past clients, and my interactions with them to find things that seemed to help me get clients and work. I began to see a pattern: there were **seven different categories** that pretty much everything successful could be categorized into. I evaluated these elements, broke them apart, and analyzed how they worked together to be so effective. I looked at them and gave them a catchy name: the **Client Magnet Method.**

(Hey, I couldn't help naming it, I guess I just like to be fancy.)

Okay, I hear you, enough chatter, let's get down to it. What actually is this thing I call the Client Magnet Method? And how can it help you grow an amazing creative freelance business?

THE 7 PARTS OF THE CLIENT MAGNET METHOD

The **Client Magnet Method** has seven parts:

Chapter 1 - Competence

Chapter 2 - Authority

Chapter 3 - Positioning

Chapter 4 - Platform

Chapter 5 - Timing

Chapter 6 - Charisma

Chapter 7 - Network

The "magic" of this system isn't that any one component or few components do all the heavy lifting. It's the power of *all* the components that work in concert *together* that are so powerful. I guess it's kind of like a seven cylinder engine, where all seven cylinders are… doing their thing. (hey, I don't know how cars work, I just drive 'em. I don't know if a seven cylinder engine is even a thing.)

With that said, here's a key factoid to keep in mind: if you really want to become a "client magnet", then **you'll want to strive to have all seven of these in place in some form.** If you settle for just having a few of them, the system isn't nearly as effective.

For example, if a prospective client sees that you have the **Competence** and **Authority** to do good creative work, but they don't believe you're **Positioned** to serve their specific interests, they may not hire you.

Or, a prospective client might see you have a **Network** of people who seem to sing your praises, but if they see you don't have a **website** or a place like that where they can view your **work**, they probably won't hire you.

Remember... your business is only as good as its **weakest** component. Ignore any one of these, and you might find yourself frustrated, thinking, *"how is it that I'm doing everything I can... and yet I still don't have the amount of clients that I want?"* You might be "maxing out" just a few areas... but if you're ignoring the others, then all that hard work isn't going to yield the results you want.

The good news is, each part of this system is easy to understand and relatively easy to put in place. And while some of them might take time to fully develop, there are things you can put into practice right now that will be MUCH better than having nothing at all. As time goes by and you work on that area patiently, bit by bit, your client base grows... and so does your success at having the creative freelance business you want.

So let's begin! First, let's look at component one of the method: **Competence**.

CHAPTER 1
COMPETENCE

How Good Are You At What You Do?

I have a personal question for you: **how good are you at the creative service you provide?**

This might sound obvious, but… in order to attract the right clients, you actually must be able to deliver clients the results they're looking for.

In other words… **you gotta be GOOD.**

I know… Captain Obvious over here.

The reason this has to be said is because many of us are under the delusion that we can win clients with just a minimum of ability in the area they're looking to hire us for. Or, what we think is enough ability but really isn't.

Often the real enemy to our success isn't the actual lack of competence, but the ***illusion*** **of competence**.

The Illusion Of Competence... And How It Keeps Us Small

The classic example of someone who is likely to suffer from the **illusion of competence** is the freshly graduated college student. Sorry to pick on you, but I was once one of you, and when I graduated I thought I was ready to take on any challenge the world chose to throw at me. It turns out, I *wasn't* ready, and when I found this out it turned out to be one of the most humbling experiences of my fledgling career.

When we're in college or art school or any other place of learning for an extended period of time, it creates a sort of "bubble effect". In the educational bubble, it's easy to convince yourself (and even easier if you have others around you to help convince you) that you know more than you actually do about the professional world outside the bubble.

Another place that I see the illusion of competence is that we might have a creative skill in *one* area while hoping we can attract clients from *another* similar but still very different area.

For example, let's say you're a **writer**. Well, there are many kinds of writers out there. Let's say you are experienced at writing short stories. You got awards for writing them, and you even won a contest back in college for a short story. Now suppose someone from an ad agency is looking for a writer (hey, that's YOU!) to write a piece of copy for a Facebook ad. You're the perfect person for the job, right?

Wrong. (Sorry to burst your bubble there!)

The kind of writing one does for ads is a completely different kind of writing. In fact, it has a name that sets it apart: **copywriting**. And it's an art unto itself. People who hire copywriters know exactly what to look for, and they will be able to see pretty quickly if you don't have it. (As an aside… copywriting is really not that hard to learn, especially if you're already a writer of some sort.)

Many creative fields are this way… the overall landscape of jobs and the people who do them can be very **fragmented**. Even within a certain creative discipline, there are a number of sub-areas of freelancers, people who hire them, and how much they're paid. Between all of these fragments of the industry, there can be a big difference in factors like what a freelancer is paid and availability of jobs.

Fortunately, the illusion of competence is easy to overcome, especially in the Information Age we currently live in. The first step to a solution is **awareness**. Simply "go down the rabbit hole" and dig into the area you're interested in learning more about. Google it, listen to podcasts, or consume whatever is out there about it. Better yet, find a working freelancer in that area and buy em'a cup of coffee while you pick their brain. You'll find pretty quickly the areas that you need to learn more about. (Who knows? You might find a sub-area or "niche" within your creative field that is in big demand but there aren't enough freelancers to meet the needs that are there. That could mean a big opportunity for you!)

Perhaps, though, the most difficult thing about shaking the illusion of competence is that it's a nice, comfy **security blanket**. It keeps us from having to stretch ourselves too much and undertake the uncomfortable act of admitting that we don't know something, and then learning how to do it.

I hope I don't sound mean here, but I've met a lot of creative pros in my career **who think they're much better than they really are**. When these people are in a larger company, they can more easily hide behind other people and stay in their comfort zone, not really growing their skills. They rely on those same old abilities and just coast along. They tend to be resistant to learning new things, and resistant to change in general. To get jobs done, we usually ended up avoiding them or going around them.

As you can imagine, it's much more difficult for these people to strike out on their own and go freelance. In order to have a viable freelancing business, you must have the **radical self-honesty** that it takes to know yourself - what you're capable of, what value you bring to your prospective clients, and your strengths and weaknesses. Only then will you be able to move forward… and to be able to grow in the areas you need to grow.

The Four Stages Of Competence

Learning the necessary skills on our journey to achieving mastery in any creative field isn't a straight, easy-to-navigate line… it's a twisty and bumpy road, filled with potholes and dead ends.

There's an interesting psychological model that was developed by Noel Burch called the **Four Stages Of Competence**, or the **Hierarchy of Competence**. I think it's great for understanding our brains – and how we think – when it comes to the different levels we progress through as we learn new skills.

Looking at the chart, we can think of learning just about anything as a progression from the bottom of the pyramid to the top.

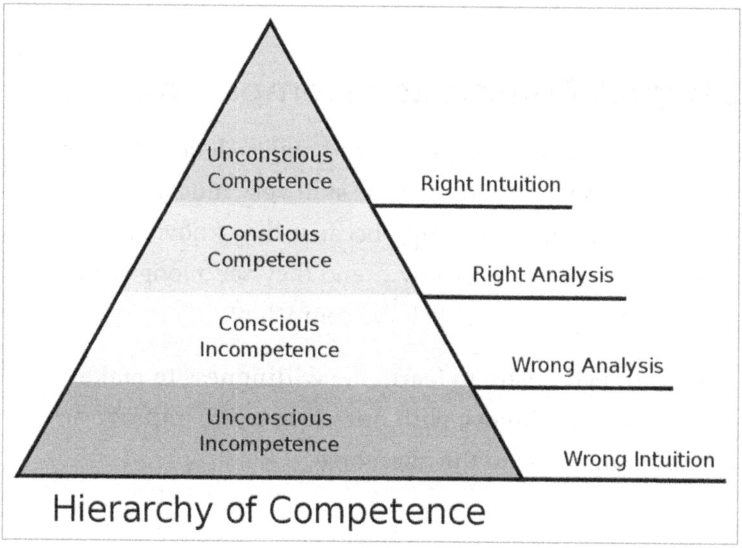

Adapted from Noel Burch by Igor Kokcharov. Creative Commons license: CC BY-SA 4.0

Stage 1: Unconscious Incompetence

In the beginning, we don't know much about how to do something… and so we don't know what we DON'T know. This is stage of Unconscious Incompetence. For example, maybe we see an artist generating amazing 3D renders or fabulous illustrations and we think, *"Hey, I'd love to be able to do that!"* We might want the **results** of gaining the skill but **we don't yet know what it takes to get there.**

In order to progress to the next stage from here, we must learn our incompetence and how much we want the new skill. The strength of our desire to learn the skill and the "honeymoon effect" of newness propels us forward.

Stage 2: Conscious Incompetence

We've realized our knowledge and ability deficit at this point, but we still haven't acquired the skill very much. This is where many people give up - because they know enough to know what they don't know... and they see a long road ahead before they are able to be competent.

The continued **desire to learn**, the **willingness to make mistakes**, and **patience with ourselves** as we improve are critical to move on to the next stage.

Stage 3 - Conscious Competence

We've reached the **basic ability to perform the skill.** We might still not be as fast as we'd like to be, and we have to "consult the manual", and think a lot about what we're doing. Doing the skill requires concentration and focus, and when this is broken, we can backslide into incompetence.

To progress to the next level, the skill must be performed more times... and as it's performed, we get better at it, and have to think less. This is where many freelancers exist in their fringe skillsets... they have an exposure to a number of different things around their main creative focus. Any one of these might be picked up and further developed over time.

Stage 4 - Unconscious Competence

The skill has been practiced enough that it has become second nature. We **don't have to think** too much about what we're doing. We make it "look easy". We might even be able to perform the skill while distracted, or in the midst of a chaotic environment.

This is **mastery**… and it's the ultimate level of competence that you should endeavor to have in your main creative skill, the one you advertise to clients and get paid to do. When you have mastery, you'll be confident when interacting with clients. You'll be able to perform under tight deadlines and stressful situations. You'll enjoy doing it, and you'll feel increasingly more confident. And… you'll be incredibly **magnetic**!

Think about it… do you enjoy watching someone who is a neophyte, the effort of concentration furrowing their brow, sweat pouring down their face, as they do something that they are new at? It's stressful! You kind of *become* them up there on stage, and like them, you hover on the uncertainty that you will be able to accomplish what you're trying to do.

On the other hand, imagine watching someone who "makes it look easy"… they have practiced the skill so many times, they are smiling and it seems like breathing to them. They even seem relaxed while doing it. You feel relaxed, too, and confident that they will be able to deliver as promised. And you marvel at the feat they're accomplishing.

Think about it: which of those two examples do you feel more drawn to? Which is more *magnetic*?

Well, that's how your clients can feel about **you**, depending on the level of competence you're achieved in your creative field.

How Do We Attain Competence?

This brings us to the actual problem of the *lack* of competence… and that, too, is a simple thing to overcome once you identify the areas you need to learn more about.

One suggestion is to **find key people** in these areas and absorb what they have to say. You may find courses you can take or even free YouTube videos and other resources that can help you. You might even find a high-level program that, while expensive, is still cheaper than the student loans you're still paying off… and promises much more targeted results. There's **never** been better access to resources to improve your skills than right now.

As you dig into an industry you might be interested in, you might find that, like one of those cool little Russian dolls, it opens up and reveals sub-industries to learn more about. The creative industries are often fractured into many different fiefdoms… and even within the area you think you know, there might be a super-specific discipline that you didn't even know about, much less be qualified for. (On the flippity-flip side, this is excellent news for those of you willing to take the time to invest in getting really good at that particular discipline… we'll talk more about that later in the upcoming section called "Positioning.")

There's an important relationship between competence and ... well, everything else. The quality of your freelance career, and I'd even say the quality of your life, depends on the level of competence you have.

When you're below average at something, it will be usually be more difficult to get clients. When you're really good at something, it will likely be much easier to get clients. (And when you're in the top five percent of your peers, you'll have to barricade your doors because clients will trample everyone in their way to get to you.)

The key to competence is to **never give up learning**. Become a lifelong learner. Never give up bettering yourself your area of creative focus. It's a marathon, not a sprint! We tend to **over**-estimate what we can do in a month…and we tend to **under**-estimate what we can accomplish in a year.

Even if you THINK you're top of the pops, look deeper… chances are, some things have come down the pipe recently in our ever-changing world that you don't know about, even if you've been in that area for years. (A.I, anyone?) We experienced freelancers aren't immune from the Illusion of Competence… in fact, we often fall prey to it because it's easy to get lazy and rest on our laurels. **Stay humble, stay sharp, and stay educated.**

There's great pleasure in being really, really good at something. It goes far beyond kudos and admiration from peers and clients. As you elevate your skills in a particular area, you'll look around and discover that you're in rare company, an elite creative pioneer discovering unexplored territory.

You'll also **enjoy your work** a lot more. You might find yourself in what's called a **flow state**, where you've been working for hours and you lose track of time. The tools and methods are so ingrained into our brains at this point that they become transparent, and we can use them without thinking about it.

Dealing With Overwhelm

The 80/20 Rule

Ok that last section, I realize, may have sounded a bit overwhelming. I hear you: *"But Mike… my brain is already full to bursting!"* Well, I have a solution for that… and a way to cut your excess brain waste to as much as 80 percent!

It's using a tried and true corollary called **Pareto's Principle**… or, as it's most commonly known, "**The 80/20 Rule.**"

This rule applies to a lot of different things in life. For the purposes of our freelancing journey, and for talking about competence in our area of expertise, it implies that around 20 percent of what we learn gets actually used about 80 percent of the time.

Competence doesn't mean going down the rabbit hole of every single detail of a program and be able to quote it like a robot. It DOES mean that you want learn the **absolutely important stuff**…the things that you will use *most*. It also means that what you do know you get really, really good at and know how to apply it practically.

So anytime you're feeling overwhelmed, use the 80/20 rule and ask yourself, *"what's the absolute necessary things that I need to know... that will give most of the results?"* You'll find the stress seep away as you realize you've just cut out 1/5 of the workload... and now the task ahead of you feels much more doable.

Focusing Just A Few Steps Ahead

Another thing that can cause the feeling of overwhelm is when we try to **look too far ahead**. We see the amount that we still have to learn to get to our ultimate goal and it intimidates us.

It reminds me of when I went on a mountain climbing trip as a teenager in Colorado. We were assaulting one of the 14,000 foot peaks of the Rockies. Being a flatlander from Texas, I was pretty inexperienced with such elevated terrain. At one point, I thought we were nearing the peak of the mountain. I couldn't see any more mountain beyond the curve that loomed ahead. By burning legs seemed to gasp, *"Finally, we're nearly there!"*

Alas, my hopes were dashed when I rounded over that curve... and saw many thousands of feet still to go.

Rather than get discouraged about the distance you are from your ultimate goal, take comfort in the smaller achievements you make along the way.

Fix your eyes on the **immediate path in front of you**... take baby steps. You can't very well solve the immediate problem if you're looking too far ahead to the hundreds of problems still waiting for you. Curate your learning to be sure you're not biting off more than you can chew... but learning the things you need most to propel yourself through the nearest tasks.

Also… don't forget to pause and **celebrate the little wins** you achieve along the way. Reward yourself. You deserve it! Many people downplay this, but I've learned that it is superbly important… you're training your brain that working smart AND working hard feels good. Show me a freelancer's happy brain, and I guarantee it will be connected to a happy (and successful) freelancer.

Competence Equals Confidence

Of course it's true that when we're good at something, we feel confident about it. This confidence seeps through every part of our freelance business. This enables us to be able to estimate more accurately how long something will take us. It will enable us to see more of the pitfalls and obstacles that we know we will face… but we will also know more about how to overcome them.

This confidence also shines through when we interact with a client. That certainty that we know how to solve their problem gives THEM confidence in YOU. They don't have control of their problem… they're looking for someone who they can trust their problem to. **That's *you*.** The more competent you are, then the more confidence you AND your client will have, and the more they will feel they can hand you the reins of the project.

Competence Does Not Equal "Project Fit"

If you try really hard to achieve competence, and you feel really good about your level of awesomeness in your niche, and yet a client doesn't award you with a job... don't get discouraged.

It could just be that the client felt like the **project** just **wasn't the right fit** for your talents. Maybe your demo reel shows that you're super-good at, let's say, drawing yellow dinosaurs. You achieve a level where you can draw yellow dinosaurs in your sleep. But then... one day you talk to a client who's looking for someone who can draw PURPLE dinosaurs. They don't want to hire you unless you show that you can draw those... silly... purple... dinosaurs.

This might sounds like a ridiculous example, and it is, but this kind of thing happens from time to time. It's amazing how many clients are in a creative industry and yet they don't seem to have much creativity... definitely not enough to bridge the "Purple/Yellow Dino Gap". They just don't seem to understand that you can do the job, even when you have confidence that you can, just because you haven't done their exact project before.

If you come up against a client's opinion that you're just not a fit for their project, don't get too bummed out. This doesn't mean that a future project won't be a fit. (It does mean that this client might want to get out of their fear-zone and open their minds a bit, but that's not our problem, is it? It's theirs.)

Now, we've talked about what competence is... let's loop back and talk about how competence fits into the Client Magnet Method.

Be So Good They Can't Ignore You

I listed competence as the first part of the Client Magnet Method because it can act as the **strong foundation** into which you build your freelance career. Being super-good at what you do gives you that strong foundation. Everything else you do will be better and easier because of it.

As you achieve more competence in your field, you'll not only have the satisfaction of being in "rare air", someone who is at the top of their game, you'll also get the **confidence** that comes with it. That confidence will ooze into every interaction and every aspect of your daily life, and you will practically *radiate* it… and as you can imagine, this makes you **incredibly attractive** to clients.

When you go into any kind of client interaction with the easy confidence that comes with competence, clients can practically *smell* it. And they are **attracted** to it like cats to catnip. Or mice to cheese. Or Cookie Monster to… well, you get the idea.

With enough competence, your **effectiveness will increase** because you'll be able to talk the talk and speak your clients' lingo. You'll be able to address their needs effectively. In fact, in many cases you'll even know what your client needs *before* they ask for it. After one conversation or email interaction with you, they'll quickly see that you're the person they want… and *need* … for the job.

The last thing I want to say about competence is to leave you with a quote to inspire you. One of my creative heroes, the great comedian, actor, and bluegrass banjo player Steve Martin once said:

> ***"Be so good they can't ignore you."***

So... strive to have so much competence oozing out of your pores that you're practically "un-ignorable".

If you do, you'll have clients for life.

CHAPTER 2
AUTHORITY

Authority: The Business Of Showing You Mean Business

The Importance Of Trust

It's important to remember that any time we come into contact with a new person that might hire us, usually **we're starting from square one** with that person. They don't know us from Adam (or Eve). And with the element of trust at an all-time low these days, we need to **earn** that trust each and every time we prospect for a new client. Sure, it sounds tedious… but it's absolutely **necessary** if you want to be able to stand out from the crowd as an A-list freelancer.

In fact, it's a good idea to imagine that each prospective client, the moment they become aware of you as a person who might be able to help them, has a special device installed in their brains. This device is called a **Trust-O-Meter**… and it has YOUR name on it. (Doesn't that make you feel special?)

Each Trust-O-Meter has a **starting amount**, which varies depending on how that person generally views the world.

(Really cynical folks who have been burned repeatedly in the past often start near zero, or even in the negative! But be patient with them, because believe it or not – these people often turn out to be the **best** clients.)

In any case, usually that starting trust amount is pretty small, and you only have one or *maybe* two chances to raise that level up. When the level in the Trust-O-Meter raises to a certain level, then they cross over into a **state of trust**.

The "State Of Trust"... And Why It Matters

This **"state of trust" is your ultimate goal.** It means that your client has made the decision that you can do the work they need you to do, and that they're comfortable with hiring you. Congratulations! You no longer have to work to earn that trust… you have it. (You do, however, need to continue to work to KEEP it! Fortunately, *maintaining* the state of trust is easier than earning it.)

This earning of trust might all sound very daunting… after all, when we say we can do something, why don't people just believe us? Why shouldn't people just trust each other more? (Hmm… have you viewed your inbox lately? Mine is filled with emails from places claiming to be reputable organizations that I use all the time… but it's not them, it's scams. That's just the world we live in.)

Yes, it takes work. And the sooner we realize it, the sooner we can get on with this business of building trust. The good news is, you can **leverage a number of tools** to do the heavy lifting of earning that trust for you. If you create the right materials and **Authority Elements**, and set them up correctly, then the actual contact with your prospective client is pretty much a breeze.

You see, **clients WANT to trust you.** They WANT you to be the person who rises to the top of their list. They WANT nothing more than a reliable freelancer that they can work with, and who they can call on over and over. If you can do the work, and they need the work done and can pay for it, then your mutual goals are aligned… you just have to get through these preliminary trust-building stages first.

...Clarity Helps, Too

Before I list them, one more thing to keep in mind about your Authority Elements is that it's important to be crystal-clear on exactly what you do, and on the **results** you provide. Your client needs to be able to see that you can do the work they need done. You're not the only one who has to prove it… they might have to prove it, too… to their superiors.

And as you'll see, it's just as critical to vet out the clients who **aren't** right for you as it is to attract the ones who **are**. When done right, these materials act as a sort of "filter" for your business… letting the good clients in while keeping the "lame"ones out. (Isn't it empowering when you realize that the client isn't the only one making a choice… that YOU also have the power to choose *them*?)

So… what are the **Authority Factors** that you can use to 1. Build trust and 2. Filter the correct clients?

Here's a list, in no particular order (although the top three are the most important):

Authority Factors For Creative Freelancers

1. Body Of Work

"How do I host my body of work online?"

If you don't have a personal website to host your reel or portfolio yet, that's okay… for now. (I do strongly recommend one, for reasons I'll talk about when we get to the section on websites).

You *can* use a file-sharing platform such as **Dropbox** or Apple **iCloud** or Microsoft **OneDrive** to host your body of work… but I don't really recommend it, because these methods don't give you much control over how your work is presented.

You could use a portfolio-based site such as **Behance** which is an Adobe platform, and you get a Behance website whenever you subscribe to Adobe Creative Cloud. While this is going to be within the Adobe ecosystem, with other links to things all around including other artist websites, this is great if you're just starting out and its better than no website at all.

For demo reels, since they're video-based, **Vimeo** is a good choice. I like Vimeo better than YouTube because Vimeo's interface is clean, with no ads (YouTube is always experimenting with different ads throughout their videos, and you have very little to no control of how and when they are shown, as well as the ads themselves.) Vimeo even has a free tier which has a limited amount of storage, but since your reel will just be a few minutes long at most, this shouldn't be a problem. Vimeo is where I currently host my demo reel, and I've had a great experience with it.

There are a number of options, more than I've listed… just be sure the method you choose to show your body of work is clean, free of visual clutter and ads, and quickly accessible so that your clients only focus on YOU, not a new pair of pumps or an annoying pop-up ad. They shouldn't have to wait a long time for it to load, or they may give up and go to their next candidate in line.

I like to think of your body of work like a piece of art in a **museum**… with plenty of space and nice clean white walls so that the your artwork is the center of attention. Anything else takes away from your prospective client's experience… and lowers the odds that they will stick around and look at your work.

Your online hosting method should also be something that you will feel comfortable **updating** regularly as you create more work and complete more successful client jobs. If you have to jump through a bunch of technology hoops just to add your most recent freelance gig, then you probably will find yourself avoiding it, which isn't a good thing!

How do I build and organize my body of work?"

Your presentation should ideally tell a **story**… it should have a cohesive flow, with a beginning, middle, and end. It should only contain your **best** work, with your absolute best pieces bookending the presentation at the very beginning and end… so you can start strong and end strong.

If there are any projects that would require any kind of explanation, such as:

"I did this when I was just a freshman in school, so I didn't quite know how to hold the mouse yet!"

Or:

"This could have been better, but let me tell you all the stuff I went through to even get to this point!"

… then it's best to skip that one. **Your pieces should be able to stand alone, without any explanation.**

"How much work should I include?"

Your portfolio or demo reel should have enough of a sampling to show what you can do… but it shouldn't be too long, or your viewer will get bored and move on.

For newer creatives with less work under their belt, you can include student work or personal work to fill out your repertoire, but only if it's top notch. Student work really just has one purpose when created: to help you learn. The learning process rarely generates the kind of refined quality you want in your Body Of Work. If you really want to use it, it probably **needs be reworked** to be the high quality that your Body Of Work requires. Remember, we don't want to just complete an assignment here… we want to be *magnetic*!

"Are Personal Projects Okay To Include?"

Personal work is fine to include in moderation, it shows your imagination and that can stretch your creative muscles. Just be sure it's still on-theme with the rest of the work in your reel… for instance, aspiring industrial designers shouldn't just have a lot of personal projects that are of 3D animated T-Rexes. Even if those dinosaurs are nearly good enough to be in the latest *Jurassic Park* movie, it communicates to the client: *"I don't really* want *to do industrial design, but hey, it pays the bills!"*

For those of us who are more… ahem, *seasoned* creatives… who possess a large body of work, consider leaving out those older pieces that might show their age. Yeah, maybe they were for a big brand and they were cool at the time, but if you have too many of these your clients may be saying *"well, what have they done* ***lately****?"* Technologies and styles change, and they will feel out of date, no matter how cool they may be… and if your work looks out of date, your client will think YOU are out of date.

"What If I've Lost All Objectivity, And I'm Stuck On What I Should Put In?"

Are you at a loss as to what you should include? A valid question. Sometimes we lose objectivity about our work because we're too close to it. For example, there are certain projects that I've done that I'd rather not see again… not because of their lack of aesthetic value, but because I revised them a lot, it was a frustrating experience, and was just ready to move on! Other projects are the opposite… I have a fondness for them because they were the first time I learned a new skill, or I have good memories of that time period. These **emotions can contaminate** our opinions about our work.

The solution is to find a few people you trust… preferably, people in your creative industry… and ask them which pieces you should include if there's any doubt. (Usually, if there's any doubt, it's best to shelve them… or if you hate doing that, earmark them for improvement later if it's feasible.)

Whew, that was quite a… body of work… about your body of work! On to the next authority factor:

---

2. Resume

Your **resume** (or C.V., in some circles) lists in a brief, succinct manner your qualifications for the gig you're trying to get.

Granted, it's kind of an old-school construct for an age when people had file cabinets so that they could stuff papers in them. Or desks that acted as a platform for stacking papers on. You might disregard the need for a resume, thinking that the people you'd want to work with wouldn't care about such a thing.

Well, you might be right… but the trouble with ignoring the need for a resume is that you often have **gatekeepers** in the way of you and your eventual client… and these gatekeepers must have a resume. These might be Human Resources people who have checkboxes to tick off… and if you have a big fat nothing in your checkbox by a line that says "resume", you could be shunted right off the list. These days, the gatekeeper might even be an automated process that scans your resume for keywords and puts your data in a database.

So let's humor the checklist people (and the robots) and make a **resume**. It needn't be that hard. There are a ton of resources for creating a solid resume that can help you pass even the checkiest of checkboxers out there. A Google search will reveal a wealth of templates that you can use. You might even consider hiring a Fiverr gig for this. Or, maybe try one of the A.I. resources that are out there, there are free ones that can spin you up a resume in a jiffy.

No matter whether you format it yourself or have a minion do the task, you'll still want to be sure to gather all your important data and **keywords**. Keywords are... uh... "key"... because of the aforementioned automated processes that sift through resumes... and filters those to the top that have matches for the job they're looking for. So you'll want to be sure the keywords they're looking for are in the resume.

For example, let's say you're a graphic designer. Rather than just repeating "graphic design" over and over in your resume, look at incorporating the words "typography", "layout", "Adobe", "Illustrator", "InDesign", "Brand", "Concepts", "Print", "Art Direction"and stuff like that. (Obviously, don't include them if they don't apply to you, but you get the idea.) For some clues as to what keywords are important, simply look at the client's job posting or job description, or peruse similar job descriptions.

Format it nicely and cleanly, and don't use any funky graphics or fonts. We're aiming for a professional look here, not advertising for a middle school garage band.

I noticed recently when helping my daughter with her resume that Canva has some good templates, but also a lot of templates with a bunch of extra stuff like a place to upload your portrait. I wouldn't do that, just keep it simple.

As for length, try to keep it to **a page or two**. Be sure to make it a .pdf file, because any other file format like a .doc file could get re-formatted and scrambled into unrecognizable goo by the time it goes through your prospective employer's unmerciful machines.

3. References

Getting a few solid professional **references** rounds out my "must have" trio of Authority Factors. This is the easiest of the three to do… and yet it might to be the one that the fewest people actually do.

This is because we may be nervous about asking people to act as references. I get it, it's kind of awkward… if you think of it in "you" terms.

From the perspective of the person being asked, they're actually probably going to be flattered that you chose them and trusted them with such a responsibility.

Still nervous about asking someone for a reference? Not to worry, I'll give you a quick little script that you can adjust however you like. Let's say the person you're hitting up is named Billy Jo.

"Hi, Billy Jo! I hope you're doing well. I was just wondering if you wouldn't mind if I put you as a professional reference for potential

clients who are looking to hire me. If not, then that's okay, I completely understand… but if so, then would you mind sending me your current email and phone for my records? Thank you so much! I really appreciate it. Best regards - Mike"

Just reword however you see fit… and do throw in a little personal bit of course, if applicable. Maybe you remembered that client was into F1 Racing or collecting butterflies or competitive axe-throwing, and you throw in something about that. Make it personal!

Do this **three times**… and voila! You have **several strong references**. Put it on your calendar to keep up with your references once a year or whenever you see fit to be sure their contact info is still accurate. Your client might not even follow up on them… but then again, it might just be that last decisive thing they needed to pull the trigger on hiring you.

4. Reviews and Testimonials

Reviews and **testimonials** essentially accomplish the same thing as references (for our purposes, at least.) They're really helpful when you're trying to build authority because it proves to someone that other clients have successfully hired you and are satisfied with the results you provided them. Not only that, but they're also willing to go on record saying so!

Once you've successfully completed a job for a client, and if that client had a good experience with you, then that's the best time to ask them for a review. Don't wait too long, or the "freshness" of just finishing a job won't be as … well, "fresh".

Like references, reviews might feel a little awkward to ask for. Sure, you might feel silly asking someone for a review. But understand that for the person being asked, it's not awkward at all. The best clients value their freelancers and they want them to have healthy businesses, and they understand reviews are an important part of the process.

Here are some things that may help when asking for a review or testimonial:

- **Ask Politely.**

Tell them that you are respectful of their time, and are requesting just a few minutes to say a little bit about their experience working with you.

- **Make It Easy.**

Have an online method (such as LinkedIn or a Google Form) set up to receive the review, with a link that your client can click so that all they have to do is say a few words about how you were to work with, and your performance, and move on.

- **Ask Clear Questions.**

Your clients have a lot on their mind. Supply them with questions so that they don't have to spend their brain power formulating an answer.

Here are some ideas for specific questions you could ask:

"How Was (Your Name) to work with?"

"What qualities did (Your Name) have that made him/her successful?"

"What's an experience that stands out in particular during your time working with (Your Name)?

As already mentioned, a Google Form is great for this, and is free. Alternately, you can use LinkedIn's "Recommendations" mechanism, which actually works really well. When your person leaves their recommendation, it will automatically show up on your LinkedIn profile. To ask someone for a recommendation, you can go to your profile, scroll to the section that says "recommendations", and click on the Plus symbol. If this section isn't available, you will have to add it by clicking "Add Profile Section" at the top.

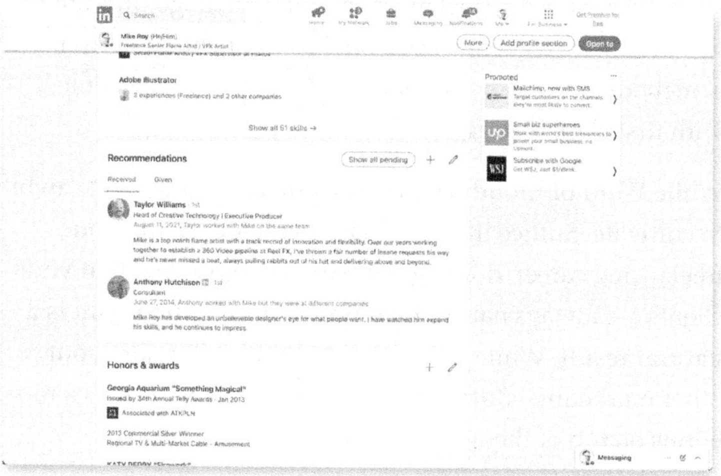

An example of the recommendations section of a LinkedIn profile

5. Word Of Mouth (or *Network*)

Don't underestimate (or ignore) the power of **Word of Mouth**. As you progress in your career, you'll find that this is by far the *easiest* way to get clients.

If reviews and testimonials are the words of other people who have said things about you, then Word of Mouth is other people (usually your past clients) **actively talking about you**... without you even being involved! The end result can be a brand new client calling or emailing or messaging you out of the blue asking for your availability to work on a project.

Word Of Mouth is so powerful, and it carries so much **built-in authority** with it, that you can even bypass the usual channels that other freelancers might have to go through to get work with a client. A personal recommendation from somebody they know shoots you directly to "clientsville", with first class seating!

While Word of Mouth is certainly powerful, it can take awhile to cultivate. Suffice it to say, that as you level up in your freelancing career, doing great work and ensuring that your clients are always happy, then **positive spin about you is a natural result.** While you certainly shouldn't ignore your other marketing efforts, word of mouth can be seen as a nice bonus on top of them.

While Word Of Mouth is an authority factor, it's *also* one of the essential elements of your Network, which we talk about later in Chapter 7... so if you're interested in how to make the power of word of mouth work for you in a more purposeful way, just keep reading!

6. Case Studies

A **case study** is an in-depth analysis or demonstration of how you helped your client achieve the creative result they were looking for.

Think of them as "deep-dives" where you talk about the full extent of a project, including ways you went about tackling the problems, challenges you overcame, and material you generated in early stages such as sketches, motion tests, or research. Case studies can take some effort to craft, but if you do this for a few of your **best** projects, it will go miles toward establishing your authority here!

These are fantastic for projects that have a unique and interesting twist to them, such as a project where you used a new cutting edge technology or platform. Or, maybe you found out a new way to do something, or you just feel really good about how a project turned out. Or, maybe it was simply just a high-profile project for a major brand or personality that you'd like to name-drop a little bit.

These are surely worth sharing in a social media post… and when you do, prepared for them to garner a bit more attention and "virality" than the normal post. People love to peek "behind the curtain" of a creative person's process, and your prospective clients are no different.

Ideally, you would host the case study on your website where you can curate the experience by making it feature-rich with images and videos so that your visitor gets a comprehensive feel of how the project came to be (and… by extension… how awesome a creative pro you are!)

While a case study may take a bit more effort to put together, it **cements your authority** in a way that few other marketing materials can. They're also much more "evergreen" than your average post, which means they can stay relevant for a very long time.

---

7. Awards

You won't have many **awards** starting out, but as you progress in your career, you may be involved with a project that gets put up for an award. When it does, congratulations... you've become an award-winning artist!

Even if it's not an award that you get individually for your specific accomplishments, the **project itself** might get an award. For larger or more high-profile projects, that award can involve a number of people. In the world I freelance in, which is mostly national commercials and at times music videos, it can involve a small army!

As a gun-for-hire, you might not immediately know that a project you worked on even gets submitted for an award. There may be an agency that hired the studio that hired you, and they put the project up for an award, and you never realize it. Every once in a while I do a Google search for a project I worked on... not every project, but maybe the more high-profile ones... and sometimes I find out that it won an award.

This goes without saying, but I should say it anyway... just be sure when you list the award on your website or post it on socials that it wasn't a project where you signed away your right to say you worked on it. Sometimes NDA (Non Disclosure Agreement) projects are like this. I've had a few projects like this that I can never talk about… which is a bummer… but hey, sometimes you gotta take the work. At least I knew going in that this was the case, and I had the chance to pass it up… or ask for more money to buy my silence.

(Yes, call me a sellout, but my silence can be bought – for the right price. I have plenty of other projects on my demo reel, I'm okay with never being able to say that I worked for a solid month for a certain fruit company that doesn't produce fruit. That's all I can say… no more questions…)

---

8. Credentials

A **credential** is an "official" record that you worked on a project, with your name attached to it in some way. (Quite the opposite of the anonymous creative month-long effort given to a certain fruit company that doesn't produce fruit… ok, ok, dropping the subject now….)

For example, freelance writers might be used to seeing their name posted at the head or at the end of an article or blog post. In fact, credit is often a **point of negotiation** when doing writing gigs of all kinds.

Long-form media projects (films, series, etc.) often list the people who worked on them in credits at the end, usually known as a "film credit". Other short-form projects like commercials might have a list of credits that's posted online. Over the years, I've built up a nice little repertoire of these projects and most of them are listed on my IMDB page. If you're not familiar with IMDB, it's the Internet Movie Database, which shows not just movies and shows but other entertainment projects such as games or other content.

Different creative niches might have their own directory or database like this, where professionals might go and see people's credentials for that niche. If you're unsure whether this kind of thing exists in your particular field, it may be worth a look.

Having a credit within a really large project might not seem like a big deal, especially when you see your tiny little name in the midst of a sea of other names… and maybe the end credit scroll of a movie or show is a bit antiquated… but I still enjoy seeing my little ol' name scroll by! Fortunately, this also carries some amount of authority with it… and it's one more little brick in your "wall of authority".

9. Education and Certifications

If you completed any **educational degrees** or **courses** that apply to the world you're freelancing in, then it's a nice authority builder. If, on the other hand, it doesn't really apply (such as that overseas study abroad program where you specialized in the study of exotic liquors) then you might consider leaving it off.

These days, information and data changes rapidly… it's more about what you've done or learned about *lately* that's more relevant than what you learned in college twenty years ago. That's good news for people who like to learn… there's no shame in continuing to take courses to improve yourself. When you do learn a new skill, display it proudly!

Certifications are an official record that you successfully passed an exam, usually after taking a vetted and approved course. This is used quite a bit by those in the tech world, such as programmers or coders… but a certification can still apply if you're using a particular software or tool to accomplish your craft. For example, companies like Adobe (Photoshop, Illustrator, After Effects, etc.) and Avid (ProTools, Media Composer) have official certification programs, as do many other industry-standard software makers. Many creative niches have a go-to software they use, and an official certification could prove to be a valuable authority booster in their eyes.

As we all know, AI is taking the world by storm, and it's affecting literally EVERY industry, including the creative ones. It couldn't hurt to take one or two of the free AI courses out there such as Google's free one on Coursera, which awards a certificate you can proudly display on your LinkedIn profile. There are also a number of free university courses you can take, hosted by distinguished bastions of learning such as MIT or Stanford. (While it's often free to 'audit' these university courses online, the official certification usually costs something.)

Education and certifications show that you care enough about your professional development to take the time to invest in courses and training to improve your skills – and to invest in yourself. And not only do you actually get valuable training, you get that 'gold star' that shows you dedicated your time (and/or money) to achieve it, and this can go a long way to building your authority in your chosen space.

10. Interviews

As you progress in your career, you may be contacted by someone to do an **interview**. When this happens, take them up on it!

Whether it's for a blog post or a podcast or a YouTube video, interviews are a great authority builder because people see that someone else considered you enough of an authority to spend time interviewing you. Like your references and client reviews, this is valuable "**social proof**", which means that someone else affirms that you are who you say you are.

To maximize the interview's effectiveness, ask for a selection of questions beforehand so that you can prepare for them. Many interviewers are experienced at getting the most out of their subjects, so the more you can prepare, the better the result.

You don't even need to necessarily wait around for an interview to happen… you can **seek them out** yourself! You can locate people in your space who do interviews, such as someone who does a podcast in your niche. Get in touch with them and let them know that you're available if they might be interested in interviewing you. Many times they have an online form or scheduling app you can fill out and set a time to do the interview.

Afterwards, capitalize on your newfound visibility by **posting the link** of the interview on your socials, making a post on your site, or sending it out in your email newsletter. You've just scored a big boost of professional authority!

11. Articles

In much the same way that interviews can give you instant authority in the eyes of your clients, **articles** can as well.

If you like writing about what you do, then this should be an easy thing to do. Even if you don't enjoy writing, you might consider looking into an A.I. language model to help, such as ChatGPT or Gemini. (I wouldn't recommend that you just copy and paste whatever it gives you – instead, use it as inspiration and/or structure, and modify it with your own words and personality.) With these amazing tools, even the most grammatically challenged of us can put out a good article, as long as we know what we're talking about.

Where do these article opportunities exist, and how can you find them? Chances are, you already know of many blogs, trade magazines, or other places that articles in your space can be found. A quick search can yield even more that you might not have known about.

These sources of articles are always looking for more content... throw your hat in the ring and let them know that you'd like to contribute. You might even get paid, but even if not, you've just built yourself a great source of authority that will live out there in perpetuity.

12. Searchability

If someone went online and typed in your name in Google's search engine, what comes up in the search results?

Or, if someone using a social platform searched for your exact freelancing niche, would you show up anywhere in their list of results?

Whether or not you're visible to the bots that crawl the web every day, hungrily scooping up data on every person that they can, is what I call your "**searchability**." And as you can imagine, the more prominent you are in that search result, the more authority you will appear to possess to your prospective clients.

I touched on this earlier when I talked about websites. While your personal portfolio website is a nice boost to your overall searchability (and the authority that automatically goes with it), there are a number of other places you might exist online. These places can include social media, trade magazine websites, blogs, YouTube, IMDB, or any number of sources.

The more places you exist online, the more likely you are to turn up in search results…and the better your "authority score". (Hopefully the majority of these results are related to the freelance work you do, and not your inebriated selfies from that crazy night in Vegas!)

One hint here: if you don't appear in the first page of Google search results at all, or if you have a plain-Jane name, then you might consider goosing it up a bit by including your middle name. Don't have a middle name (or one you like?) Invent a nickname!

I started using my middle name because there was already a comic book artist and a soap opera actor who already possessed most of the "Mike Roy" internet cred. And because I wasn't paying enough attention in the 90's, someone already snagged the mikeroy.com domain name too.

What's a guy to do?

Well, I decided to drag out that middle name my mama gave me, brush the dust off of it, and start using it. I now pretty much own the entire first page in the Google search results for "Mike Glen Roy"!

I'm by no means "internet famous"… but at least I'm more 'findable' now.

13. Published Works

A **book** you've published can go really far in showing people you know what you're talking about. The printed word (digital or otherwise) does still carry some weight.

For example, the creative studio I used to work for once hired a guy that had written a book on rotoscoping. When people would talk about him in the company, they would say, "*… and he also wrote a book on rotoscoping!*" People naturally assumed he was not only highly capable at that skill, but a thought-leader as well.

I really should separate the word "Publishing" into two different realms: "traditional publishing" and "self-publishing."

Traditional Publishing

This is when a publishing company takes you "under their wing" and shows your work on their platform or publication. It carries with it a certain degree of authority, because it shows that you've been vetted by the "gatekeepers" that are in many ways considered authorities in a certain space. A traditional publishing company might be a magazine, newspaper, or book publishing company.

This used to be pretty much the only way to get visibility on a broad scale, and with the advent of the internet and self-publishing, the landscape has changed quite a bit, so you don't necessarily have to go this route anymore to gain 'author authority'.

Self-Publishing

These days anybody can publish a book on Amazon. And, if it's niche enough, maybe the right people in a targeted market will see it. Amazon's KDP (Kindle Direct Publishing) program makes it super-easy to do this, and there are other platforms as well, such as Apple Books, Kobo, and Barnes & Noble. There are also 'aggregator' platforms that make it easy to publish multiple places at once, and the most popular one is Draft2Digital.

Sure, it's a bit intimidating when you look across the sea of books out there. There may be a LOT of books available – but there might *not* be very many books in YOUR exact creative niche. If there aren't, then self-publishing your own little ebook could be a way to skyrocket your authority in your space.

I'll prove it! Just for fun, **try a little research exercise** right now: pop open your browser, go to Amazon.com, and search for books in your exact creative niche. You might find some inspiration there, as the books that have been written for your niche might not have very many ratings or sales. Are you sniffing the sweet scent of opportunity yet?

14. Content Creation

If you enjoy writing, being on camera, or talking about what you do, then you might consider starting a blog or YouTube channel or a podcast or the like. When a potential client sees that you care enough about what you do to spend time generating **content** about it, they can't help but see you as an authority in your chosen field.

As you can imagine, as your content channel grows and you continue to develop your body of work (and your followers), your authority goes through the roof even more. In fact, a client may just treat you like something of a minor celebrity!

Sure, the "influencer culture" has given rise to a lot of people doing this nowadays, and it can feel intimidating when you look at starting your own channel when you see people out there (even people in your space) with bazillions of views. Just remember – even *they* started at the exact same place you're at right now: ground zero.

The key to becoming a content-generating machine is the thing I said at the very first of this section… you absolutely must ENJOY creating content. If you don't, then it will become a grind and you'll just give up. If you *do* enjoy it, though... you may have just found yourself a great new hobby that you not only enjoy, but that also generates you loads of clients!

15. Product Demos / Beta Testing

This might sound like an obscure one, but I included it because in my personal experience, doing a **product training demo** really did boost my career.

If you use a particular software in your creative freelancing business, you might be considered an authority on it and get some exposure that way. In my case, I did a demonstration at a user's group meeting of techniques that I had developed while creating 360 degree videos in Flame, the video effects software that I primarily use.

Autodesk, the company that makes the software, had people at that demo and they offered to pay for me to travel to a user group in New York to give the same demo. This led to doing three days of demos at the Autodesk booth at the National Association of Broadcasters conference in Las Vegas. I got a lot of amazing connections and had great conversations with people from the company, other peers, and even a couple of potential clients who were interested in working with our company.

So, if you know your software well, and if you decide to maintain a connection with the makers of that software, you could be on their radar for possible demo work or any other involvement that can help boost your authority as a user. These software companies actually value their relationships with their end users, because it provides them valuable feedback on how to make the software better. And when you succeed with it, *they* succeed as well. (You also provide them a valuable conduit to other users of the software, whom they can sell to.)

Another way to get exposure as an authority in a particular software is to join their **beta program**. Early in my career I helped beta test versions of Flame that were pre-release copies. We got free software in exchange for our input on things like bugs and suggested improvements. If you're a technically-minded person that doesn't mind a few extra bugs or crashes from time to time, then this might be a good option for you.

---

16. Newsletters

If you enjoy writing, a great authority builder, as well as a great way to stay top of mind to your clients, is to send out a periodic email **newsletter**. You would want to get your clients' permission to send them this, of course, but they will usually be happy to give you their email address if your newsletter is informative, entertaining, or beneficial to them as a member of the same industry.

I think this works really well if you're into newer, more cutting-edge areas like AI, where client education is more critical, and your potential clients may be more open to receiving news about the latest trends, developments, and technological advances.

A monthly or quarterly newsletter sent out to your email list shouldn't take too much trouble to maintain. One sent weekly certainly sounds a bit too frequent for my taste, but who knows? Feel free to do whatever works best for you and your clients.

Rather than just sending a bunch of emails directly from your Apple or Gmail or Microsoft account, I would recommend you look into using one of the email services that specialize in **email marketing**, such as MailChimp.com, who (as of the writing of this book) provide a free tier for a certain number of subscribers. You would start by uploading a list of your clients' emails, and you'd want to be sure to maintain this list and keep it updated in the event that your clients move to a different company.

MailChimp even has a number of attractive, pre-built mail templates that you can use. After composing your newsletter, they also make it super-easy to auto-fill the person's first name into your message so that your email sounds personalized just for them. When everything's ready, you hit "send" and ... voila! Your newsletter is on its way to your clients' inbox.

These mail marketing providers like MailChimp even have metrics that you can look at to see how many emails were delivered, how many were "bounced" (meaning there was no active email address), and even who opened their email... very useful stuff to know.

If I sound like a know-it-all, that's because I'm a user! I started using MailChimp way back in 2011. Since then I have also used ActiveCampaign.com. I like both, but feel free to choose which one works best for you.

There are other reliable and established options out there as well, such as Aweber.com, Sendgrid.com, and Hubspot.com, which is really more of a CRM (Customer Relationship Management) tool. In fact, much of this software blurs the lines between just doing email and being a full-fledged CRM… which can keep track of your customers data in a feature-rich database, do stuff like remind you when to follow up with them, and a load of other cool things.

17. Mailers

Good old "snail mail" isn't just for window replacement companies and credit card offers! If you decide to try this, you might just find that it can work to win some clients. There's something that feels substantial, solid, and more "real" about stuff that's **printed**. Rather than mass-sending a bunch of mailers to random people, though, you would want to try to get a list of actual addresses of people who could be potential clients.

For example, if you're a freelancer who specializes in designing and building websites for a certain kind of company, you could gather the addresses of these companies. Even better, you could find out the key person at the company and include their name in the address. As you can imagine, examples of your best work in their hands in the physical form of a real, printed card could go a long way to establishing your authority in their mind… especially if it's relevant to their business.

There are a number of services that can mail flyers or postcards with an attractive full-color print of your work.

One example is **sendoutcards.com.** A friend of mine used them a few years ago and really liked the results. You can have the cards custom printed on demand and sent in bulk for less than a couple of dollars per card. (A bit more expensive than an e-newsletter, but on the plus side, it gives those postal workers something to do!)

18. Personal Factors

Have you ever talked with someone and they just seemed like they had "it"? Perhaps they came across as someone you really enjoyed conversing with. Or maybe they made you feel like you were more important, or more special, from having talked to them. These people possess intangible qualities I'll call "**personal factors**."

Call it whatever you want... maybe it's a charisma, maybe it's the way they communicate confidently, clearly and decisively. Some people just seem to have this quality about them more than others... and it certainly goes a long way toward their perceived authority.

I won't spend a lot of time on this here, because I actually have an entire section devoted this kind of thing I call "**charisma**" later in this book. (That's how significant it is). What I think it really comes down to ... in terms of your Authority... is being able to clearly communicate, whether verbally or literally, what you do and how you do it. It's also being able to convey to your client that you can help them with the creative problem that they need solved.

We'll talk more later about this… just keep in mind that this is one Authority Factor that makes all those other factors shine even brighter, cementing you as somebody who can get the job done, get it done well, and even get it done with flair!

19. Website

I saved this one for last because I'm going to go into a bit more detail about it than I did for the other factors. This is because the concept of having my own website has a special place in my heart.

Back in the 90's when the web was a fresh, new, and yet objectively ugly thing (not unlike a newborn human), I buckled down and **learned how to build a website.** I saw the benefit of having a digital portfolio that any client could access 24/7. This turned out to be a good call… because not only did my website build my authority at a new freelancer, it also got me paid work.

Using Your Website To Attract Clients

A personal website is **your own little piece of virtual "real estate" on the web**. It embodies the spirit of freedom of the internet, and you put whatever you want on it. Where to begin? And what are some things that you can do to attract your best clients and show them you mean business?

Here are some things that you can put on your website to attract clients. Some are no-brainers and you should definitely have them on there, and some are optional and might take a bit of work, but they can yield great results. We've pretty much covered all these already in the list of

Authority Factors, but here I'll talk about any **specific** ways you can apply them on your website.

One more thing worth mentioning… if you want to be seen and ranked by search engines, then the more relevant material you have on your website, the better. The little bots that crawl around the web also tend to place a higher importance on **recency**, so the more you can keep your site up to date, the better. Don't stress out too much about it, though… if you have any website at all, you're doing better than most freelancers out there! If you don't have a site yet, just start small - with a few of your best projects - and build from there.

Essential Must-Have Pages On Your Website:

- Body Of Work
- Contact Info

Optional Pages for Your Website:

- Case Studies
- About Page
- Awards Page
- Reviews and Testimonials
- Resume
- Blog
- Contact Form
- Scheduling Page
- Social Media Links

Let's talk a bit more about these as they pertain to your website.

Body of Work

First and foremost, your website should display your aforementioned **Body Of Work**. This is the number one thing you want to get in front of a potential client visiting your site. In fact, it should be the ONLY thing a visitor sees on the first page of your site… anything else is a distraction.

We already talked about how to craft your body of work, whether it's a demo reel video or a collection of projects. For example, my own site at mikeroyartist.com shows my demo reel front and center, and if clients want to drill down and see individual projects they can always click on the side navigation, where I've separated the work into various categories.

If you're a print-based or graphic artist, your first page might look like a curated selection of "thumbnails" that represent a handful of your best projects. These thumbnails don't have to show the entire project, but rather are highly attractive images that invite the viewer to learn more. When a visitor clicks a thumbnail, they could be taken to a page dedicated to the project where you display more images of the project, write-ups, or even **Case Studies**.

Contact Info

It goes without saying, your clients need to have a way to get in touch with you so that they can hire you… especially after you've done all that hard work to put your accomplishments on your website!

This can be as simple as a bit of text with your email and phone number. Optionally, you can also put links to where you can be contacted elsewhere on the web, including icons that link to your active social media pages.

You can also create a **Contact Form** that has text input areas where clients can ask a question directly and leave their contact information. Depending on how this is implemented on your site, it goes directly to your email, and you get an email with the client's information. I've gotten a number of jobs this way, with a client inquiring about availability right there on my site, and it goes directly to my email inbox. Contact forms are great because it removes the step of a client manually having to tab over to their email to compose a message to you… they can do it right there from your site.

Your contact info should ideally be accessible from every single page of your website so that your clients don't have to click around to find it.

Other Pages

Many of these have been discussed, but as for their implementation on your website, they can look however you like. We'll talk in the next section a bit about the tech and ways you can implement this stuff, but I'll make a few notable notes here about a few of them.

Case Studies / Awards / Reviews and Testimonials

These content pages are great for showcasing your accomplishments. **Case Studies**, as mentioned, can be pretty detailed and take a bit of work. Your website has the rich-media capabilities to display videos, animated gif's, text areas, and images to build your case study.

An **awards** page can be a pretty simple page that lists the various awards you've achieved… and shouldn't take too long to create. Likewise, **reviews and testimonials** that your clients say about you can be copied and pasted so those should be pretty easy to make as well, while going a long way toward building your authority.

About Page

You can use an **About Page** to list a writeup of your accomplishments, your journey on how you came to be the amazing creative pro that you are today, or whatever you want! You can put pictures of yourself in action, or even pictures of you with your family, pets, or doing hobbies you love.

This can go a long way to putting a person behind the portfolio, and really draw your potential clients to you. In fact, a well written about page might just be the thing that puts you over the top and propels them decide to give you that important project! Do you have a three-legged rescue doggo named Tripod? Well then, put the little fella in your About Page! Tripod won't mind, especially if you use the extra income to buy him those exotic refrigerated treats he likes.

Resume Page

Your Resume Page is, obviously, where you would provide access to your professional C.V. or Resume.

You can display your resume nicely formatted on the page, and you can also provide a link to a .pdf file. Whether or not you decide to put your entire resume on a dedicated page, I recommend providing it as a **downloadable pdf**... otherwise, the formatting of the resume on the page might not look good when saved or printed directly from the page.

Blog

Blogs might sound so early 2000's, but they can still go a long way toward cementing your authority in the minds of your clients. If you enjoy writing, then they're a great addition to your site. In addition, you can use what you write here on social media posts, content sites such as Medium or Substack, or wherever you can put content that might generate an audience.

So what do you write about on your blog? Anything you want! Although, I do recommend that since the goal of your website is to get clients, you should focus your efforts on what's relevant to that goal. That means rather than using your professional site to rant about your views on politics, religion, or the over-use of pumpkin spice during the last three months of the year, you should write about topics that are relevant to your profession. (If you have to vent and rant, then feel free to do that... just not here!)

Here are some idea prompts:

- Thoughts on the current state of your industry (try to be positive)
- How you got through a particularly challenging aspect of a job
- Talking about a recent user group visit where you learned some new skills
- Reiterating what you learned about a new training course you took

- Your philosophies on how you work to give clients amazing results

These are just some ideas I threw out off the cuff… sit down and brainstorm some more, and I'm sure you'll come up with a pretty comprehensive list in no time. Hey, you're the expert!

Choosing Your Custom Domain Name

The holy grail of cyber-ownership is the vaunted **domain name,** or **URL**, which is your virtual "address" on the web. It's easy to do a search for available domain names… I like to use instantdomainsearch.com. Or you can use one of the many domain name providers that are out there, such as godaddy.com, or domains.squarespace.com.

If your name isn't available as a domain name (most people's isn't by this point in the internet age) then you can brainstorm modifiers that are applicable to your niche.

For example, if "**BillyJo.com**" isn't available (yes, I can't get him off my mind) then he can look into "**BillyJoCreative.com**", "**BillyJoWrites.com**", or "**BillyJoArtist.com**". The "**.com**" is known as a TLD (meaning "top level domain") and is the most common. The good old .com still carries the most authority, but will probably require an additional bit of imagination to get a URL that works well.

On the other hand, you might go with an alternate TLD like **.co** or **.net**. These are still pretty widely used, and it might not be as difficult to find with your "first name last name" formula intact. "**BillyJo.net**" still sounds like it has pretty good authority, even if it's not a .com TLD, because the name is still fully intact.

Alternatively, you might choose to use one of the newer TLD's that might fit into your creative niche. If your niche is used to seeing a ".tv" TLD like the world of motion and video is, then that's good.... and If Billy Jo does video production or motion graphics for commercials, then "**BillyJo.tv**" does the trick nicely. Just do your research when looking for these newer, lesser known TLD's… if you see plenty of others in your field using it, or even your client, then you're good!

There's one more thing about domain names to keep in mind. There is a **hosting** company that provides your domain name, and this company doesn't necessarily have to be the same company that hosts your actual website. You don't have to worry about this for now if you don't have one… if you're starting from scratch, you can get a domain name from the same company that hosts your site. There is a basic fee (usually paid annually) to host your domain name.

I used to use Google Domains for this, which was only $12 per year, and as of this writing, **Squarespace** took over their domain hosting duties and raised the cost a bit, but not too much. You can find them over at domains.squarespace.com.

How To Host Your Website

- Hosted Websites

Hosted websites are websites as a "pre-packaged service" that you pay a company to host and to some degree manage for you. After logging in, you may get to choose how your website looks, choosing from a pre-built selection of themes and even some degree of customization. All the behind-the-scenes technical stuff is taken care of for you, so all you have to worry about is the actual content on your site.

Here is a list of some popular hosted website providers (In fact, you may have seen the first couple of these advertised in commercials, that's how mainstream they are):

- Squarespace.com
- Godaddy.com
- Wix.com
- Wordpress.com

What are the *advantages* of hosted websites?

- These are great if you consider yourself a non-DIY person, or you try to avoid technology at all costs! You just want something that you can easily access, update your site, and it all just works.
- The technicals and the back-end stuff is all taken care of for you.
- They focus on making it super-easy to set up your website, and you can get one up very quickly.

What are the possible *disadvantages* of hosted sites?

- All of these services mentioned charge a subscription fee except for Wordpress.com, that one is free for the basic plan. (But when you look at the cost of a website vs. what it would cost to have an actual brick and mortar store as the storefront for your business, the price is negligible! So that's not really a disadvantage, in my opinion.)
- You may be somewhat limited in options, features and customizations compared to self-hosted sites. For example, if you want to have a fancy customized form, you might run into a roadblock there. Or, if you

decide for example that you want to implement something like e-commerce where people can purchase things from you via your website, you might see a limitation, or it might be a paid upgrade to do so.

- Your site design and contents usually aren't portable to another hosting service… if you decided to move your site, you would likely need to rebuild it.

- *Self-Hosted Websites*

In the old days (there I go again, talking about those!) self-hosted websites meant you actually had a computer in your house that was connected to the Internet and that had your website on it. Now, it almost always means you have a computer that lives on the cloud, somewhere out on the internet, and this gives you a platform that you can build whatever you want on. You still have a site to log into, but instead of automatically logging into something that already looks like a website, you have to actually put the website on there yourself.

If that sounds confusing, and you're trying to figure out the difference between this and what we just talked about in the last section, think of it this way, using the analogy of "virtual real estate": *hosted* websites are like buying a pre-built house that's already on a piece of land. By contrast, *self-hosted* websites are like renting raw land, and you have the house custom-built from the ground up. Hopefully that's a bit more clear!

If that last thing sounds like rocket science, it's actually not too bad. There are so many pre-built solutions out there for this that it's relatively easy once you invest a little time learning how to do it. The process here is that you go to a web host, sign up for a subscription, and then after logging in you choose your domain name (or you can port over a domain name from somewhere else if you wish.) Then you have a selection of things you can install on your web platform. The most popular thing by far that people choose is an application called **Wordpress** to build your website with.

"Wait a minute", you think, *"Isn't that the same thing as Wordpress.com?"*

Nope. Wordpress.com is actually hosted for you which is why is was in the list of hosted sites… while **Wordpress** (whose URL is Wordpress.org) is open source software that you can use to build a website on a self-hosted platform.

Wordpress installs with a click of the button, and then you have a new login called a Wordpress login… this takes you directly to your website. Now, from there you will want to choose a theme for your site. The Wordpress ecosystem is large and very well supported, so you have a ton of options here, from themes to how your site looks to various plugins you can use to extend your site's functionality.

You used to have to stay on top of updating your Wordpress installation regularly, as well as updating any plugins that you've installed. The ecosystem is so mature at this point, though, that all that is pretty much automated now, especially if you use a well-known web host. The better ones are actually optimized for Wordpress, so they'll have no problem with this.

Here is a list of some popular providers for web hosting where you can self-host your website:

- Godaddy.com (yep, they do both hosted and self-hosted)
- Bluehost.com
- Siteground.com (the one I use, and my favorite of the bunch!)
- Hostinger.com
- Dreamhost.com

***Advantages* of self-hosted websites are:**

- Freedom! You get to put whatever you want on the site. (Well, as free as the laws of where you reside allow you to be, anyway)
- Unlimited customizations with plugins (or you can even hire your Uncle Earl who is a web coder to add features to your site if you want).0
- You have much more control of how your site looks with a virtually unlimited selection of free and paid themes.
- The subscription is typically cheaper than hosted websites, as little as a few dollars a month.
- Wordpress is free, as are many of the plugins and themes for Wordpress.
- The tech to host your site is well established and not too difficult to learn, if you use Wordpress.
- Portability: if you decide to move to a different web host, you can package up your entire site and migrate it without too much trouble.

Possible *Disadvantages* of self-hosted websites:

- It's not as cut and dried or simple as Hosted Sites, and requires a bit more knowledge.

- You are responsible for updating and managing your website behind the scenes (although, as was mentioned, this is becoming less and less an issue with automation and tech support).
- If you don't stay on top of updates, there's an off-chance that you might be vulnerable to a plugin or feature that could be hacked if you have an older bit of tech that has been exploited in some way.

Becoming An Authority In Your Field

This section on Authority, its importance, and how to build it was quite a large section in our exploration of the Client Magnet Method! **Let's summarize** the points we talked about.

It's not enough for us just to be good at something… we also have to be able to **show** it. While competence is your ability to do a creative task, **authority** is *proof* that you can do it. You show your prospective clients your authority by a number of **Authority Factors.**

These Authority Factors can be a number of things that show you can help your prospective client achieve a specific creative result. There are a lot of options to choose from, but there are several that I listed as being bare-bones essential things to have, and those are **Body Of Work**, **Resume** (or CV), and **References**.

Your **Body Of Work** does a lot of the heavy lifting, as it shows the best examples of your work - and it's a great idea to put some effort into this, as well as keep it up-to-date as you complete jobs. While a **resume** might be considered an aging artifact of a bygone era, many clients still like to have one on file, and they are essential for applying to many gigs online. Your list of **references** are essential because new clients might ask for it, as it gives them actual humans that they can ask about you, and this skyrockets their trust in you as well as your authority.

Speaking of trust, we also spent some time talking about the importance of **trust** and how important it is for winning the hearts and minds of your clients. When you reach the goal of being in a "**state of trust**" with a client, it's much easier to win freelance jobs and be the go-to resource for future jobs.

As for the other authority factors we discussed, here is a rundown: **Reviews and Testimonials, Word of Mouth, Case Studies, Awards, Credentials, Education and Certifications, Interviews, Articles, Searchability, Published Works, Content Creation, Product Demonstrations, Newsletters, Mailers, Personal Factors,** and **Website.** Whichever additional ones you choose to pursue should be chosen and crafted to put you in the best possible light, maximizing your strengths.

Considerable time was given to the last factor on the list, a **Website**, since I strongly recommend that every freelancer have one, due to its many benefits. These pluses include being able to get "free" exposure via search engines, as well as being a place you can control that houses your Body Of Work and many other Authority Factors you may choose to show there.

The time and effort you invest in building your authority, especially in things that yield outsized results compared to the effort that's required, can make a **massive difference** in your creative freelancing career. Having authority in your space can make every other aspect of your freelancing **easier**... leading to more trust from your clients, less need to "hustle" client prospects for jobs, and – eventually – a more robust bank account!

A Final Note To Prevent Overwhelm

I know what some of you *might* be thinking after reading this section of the book:

> *"I feel so overwhelmed! I actually have to do all of this?"*

No. Absolutely not.

The **top three are the most important** (Body of Work, Resume, and References). I would recommend that every freelancer does those. (I also put in a plug for a website because I feel while it's not absolutely necessary, it *is* very beneficial in many ways.)

As for the others (and after you've already done the three main ones), **pick one** that feels like something you'd be interested in doing. Follow the steps to incorporate that into your business. You can always change later, or even add another Authority Factor at your leisure.

Remember: the single point of failure in your business is YOU. So It's important to choose Authority Factors that you'd be able to follow through with. Choosing **one** of these and working on it a little bit each week is better than choosing ten of them and working for a month and then giving up.

And, don't forget... to **have fun** while doing it!

CHAPTER 3
POSITIONING

How To Be "Seen" (And Not Just Part Of The Scenery)

Have you ever tried to find something in a dimly lit room? I did, just the other day. I fumbled around for a while and eventually my toe. It was NOT a pleasant experience. When I wisely turned the light on, I was able to find what I was looking for… and I found it much more easily. (I was even able to find the newly needed band-aids, too!)

If you want to become magnetic to your clients, then **they have to be able to see or notice you.** You have to "turn your light on".

And seeing is just the *first* part. After they notice you, they have to be able to **define** exactly what it is that you do… so they can decide whether you can help them or not, and take the next step with you (or not). This is why positioning yourself in your marketplace is so critical to your success.

The key to both getting noticed and being "definable" by

your position in the marketplace so that your clients can find you is ***specificity***.

The Power of Specificity

We creative freelancers often possess a diverse skill set. It's fun to be able to say we know a lot of different things. Hey, we earned it!

But while it's cool that we can do a lot of things, in our freelance business, it's crucial to be able to narrow that down - to define and communicate a specific **niche** that we're good at providing value in. **Clients are drawn to *specialists* who demonstrate a deep understanding of their specific needs.**

For example, imagine a client looking for a graphic designer. The choice between a generalist designer - someone who has some flyers, logos, layouts, package design, and a little bit of everything else - and a designer specializing in the **exact thing** they're looking for is clear. **Specificity** not only helps freelancers attract the right clients but also allows us to command higher rates by positioning ourselves as **experts** in our chosen field.

What Ocean Are *You* Swimming In?

The **Blue Ocean Strategy**, coined by W. Chan Kim and Renée Mauborgne, encourages businesses (including freelancers) to explore untapped markets - "blue oceans" - instead of competing in crowded "red oceans."

In the **red ocean,** where competition is high, freelancers often find themselves battling on price. Clients may view services as interchangeable, making it difficult to command top pay rates. As a result of being in a crowded market, there's tremendous pressure to lower rates. Not only that… it's very difficult for a freelancer to stand out and be unique.

Conversely, the **blue ocean** is a market that's not crowded with a lot of other freelancers who provide the same creative service. This allows us to focus on delivering exceptional value, creating a space where we are the go-to experts. Since freelancers here are less in supply, we can also expect less competition – as well as higher rates.

To transition from the red to the blue ocean, freelancers **must identify what sets them apart**. This could be a unique style, a specialized skill, or a particular approach to projects. It could also be experience for a particular segment of a market. The goal is to **make the competition irrelevant** by **offering something that others don't.**

What About Purple Oceans?

Considering this strategy, and reflecting on my own experience, I personally think the ideal reality is somewhere in-between…a *Purple* Ocean Strategy, if you will.

What I mean by this is, sometimes you can be SO niche, so far out there in unique-land, that nobody is aware of your existence. That blue ocean looks mighty lonely, doesn't it? On the other hand, perhaps you can benefit from a bit of the blue ocean, where you're unique and you can fill a specific need… while also having "a red-tinted" market that has enough of a demand (and a supply) for freelancers just like you.

Furthermore, creative markets like ours (as you probably know by now) often overlap with other markets. And… as all us creatives know… red mixed with blue makes purple!

All this talk of markets can be confusing if you don't have a **framework** in mind of how they can relate to each other… and what your place might be within those markets, looking for where you can fill a need.

Example: My Own Niche

As an example of how to look at different creative markets, and even build a mental framework for understanding them, let me tell you about my own creative niche, which is "Flame Artist" or "Finishing Artist". I'm aware that the average person, even the average creative freelancer, has no idea what those words mean. But I know from experience that **my clients know exactly what they mean**, they know the **value** I provide, and they search for me by those ***exact* keywords.**

My main niche exists as a sub-niche of what you can call "Commercial Post Production" which itself is a subset of the "Advertising" market. 80-90 percent of the time I use color, visual effects, and motion graphics to finish commercial projects, and I mostly use a software called Flame.

Below is a diagram of some of the sub-markets within the overall market of Advertising, and where my particular niche tends to be. I might occasionally do work for a Brand or an Agency, or even a Production company… but Post-Production companies (also known as studios) are my "bread and butter".

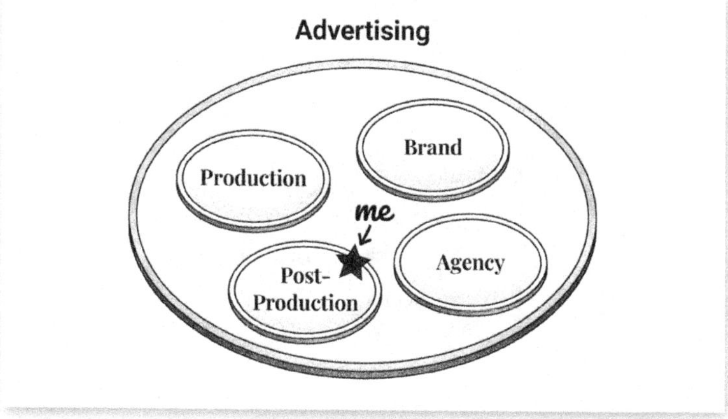

That's my main market niche, but there are significant overlaps with another broader market: the "**Entertainment" market.** This market has companies that do post-production, too. For these folks, I use much of my same skillset and software… but for different kinds of projects, like movies, music videos, show openers, and other "non-commercial" content.

These clients might not know me as a Flame artist, or know what Flame is… but they know the **result** they want. They might be looking for a "effects artist" or "finishing artist" or even a "visual effects supervisor". And for them, I might not even use Flame but another software that I also know really well and that I'm qualified for.

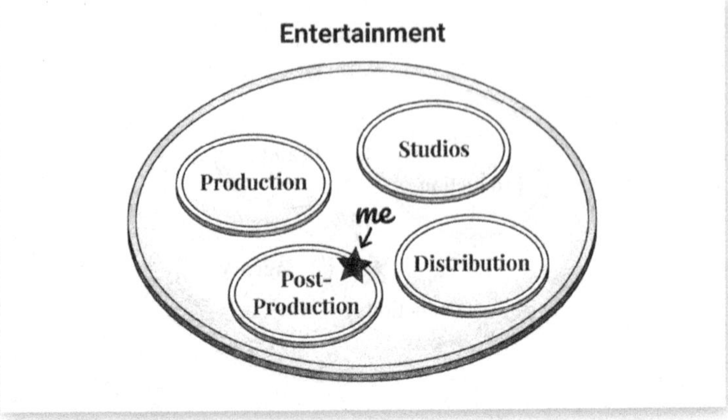

This also can illustrate the importance of knowing the lingo of what the different clients in your niche may be called. For instance, earlier I mentioned that much of my work is for smaller post-production houses in the advertising market, which many people call "studios". However, in the macro sister-market of entertainment, the word "studio" has a very different meaning… and it means the big mega-companies that make mass-market content, like Disney or Paramount.

These are simple diagrams, and they don't quite do justice to the litany of clients that are out there… but it gives an idea of how you can frame the structure in your mind.

Know Your Market (And Its Neighbors)

If you were to draw a diagram of your own creative market and its sub-markets, what would that look like? Does it give you any ideas of adjacent markets or similar ones that might look for your skills? Take some time and research your niche now. Map out the different players in your market space, their names, and what they do.

To be a magnetic freelancer, **you need to know the business you're in - the part of the ocean you're swimming in - inside and out.** This means knowing your clients... and *their* clients as well. It also helps to know the markets adjacent to yours so that you can widen the net and attract clients who need those same skills.

So WHAT you DO might be more specific... but WHO you do it FOR might vary a bit. Think of a **magnet**... it exists in one place, but it can attract from multiple directions. We'll dive more into the WHO pretty soon, because the "who"... your clients, who you will be working for... are a big deciding factor on how you position yourself.

Understanding Your TRUE VALUE As A Freelancer

It's important to understand your **true value** as a freelancer who possesses a creative specialty and a set of skills that can be put to good use in the business world. This understanding will help you in many ways as a creative pro.

This is essential because if you don't understand your value, you might think your skills are worth *less* than what the market dictates... and if this is the case, you might *accept* less. This mistake can cost you dearly over the years as you negotiate your rate!

Let's say, for instance, that you accept $100 dollars *less* per day than whatever the average rate is for your creative skill. Multiply that out by all of the days you work per year as a freelancer. Let's assume you get gigs for a just a fourth of the days in the year, that's 365 days divided by four, which gives you a total of 91 days you worked. That $100 multiplied by 90 days is $9,100 dollars... which is the amount you COULD have made ... without even getting any additional work or clients! It adds up, doesn't it?

And this is even assuming you're just working approximately 3 out of the 12 months of the year. Feel free to plug in the numbers for yourself... as you begin to get a grasp of the numbers, you'll be more equipped to think in these terms... and more able to hang in there when discussing your rates with potential clients.

As someone who's been on the client side of things, I've spent time helping choose and hire creative freelancers myself. And I can tell you with certainty that a list of high-quality freelancers - people who you have confidence in that can do the creative work they say they can do - is **worth its weight in gold**. Having this list of freelancers might even make the difference between a company being able to take a job worth hundreds of thousands of dollars ... or, depending how big the project is, possibly millions of dollars! Without that list of freelancers, they may have to pass on the job... and the gains from it.

You see, **understanding the economics and the staffing needs from the client side of things**... even just a little bit... is incredibly empowering to you as a freelancer. When you grasp this, and you begin to realize the worth of your skills, you'll have confidence and certainty... not just when it comes to quoting your rates, but in other areas as well.

Economic Impact on Freelancing Niches

Understanding the **economic dynamics of their niche** is crucial for creative freelancers. Economic trends, industry shifts, and technological advancements can significantly impact the demand for specific services. **Staying informed** about these factors allows freelancers to adapt their positioning and offerings accordingly.

For instance, during **economic downturns**, companies may be more inclined to **outsource** creative work to freelancers rather than hire full-time staff. On the flip side, economic prosperity may lead to an increased demand for premium creative services as businesses invest in enhancing their brand image. Keep an eye on the macro environment and broader economic factors going on, and you'll be better informed about how those things affect your freelancing market.

Is there a "price difference" when it comes to the different creative work you do? *Absolutely*. There's also a difference in price between people who might do very similar work but who do it for different kinds of clients and markets. For example, in the commercial market that I just talked about, clients tend to pay more than the entertainment market... even though the creative services I provide to both markets may look very much the same.

Sure, some creatives might consider taking more money for advertising clients "selling out"... after all, insurance, car batteries, or bowel movement enhancing pharmaceuticals isn't exactly sexy... but it sure goes a long way towards paying the bills! (And it keeps you 'in the game' to be able to take those "sexy" jobs when they *do* present themselves.)

Ultimately, you'll need to **strike a balance** that you're comfortable with, often between work that pays well but is less inspiring and doesn't look as good on your demo reel, and work that is inspiring and reel-worthy but may pay less. (Once in a blue moon, you'll come across a "unicorn job" that has *all* those benefits, and you'll know them when you see them… and they're worth going all-out to get!)

The Laws of Supply and Demand in Freelancing

The universal laws of **supply and demand** play a pivotal role in determining freelancers' earning potential. In niches with high demand and limited supply of skilled professionals, (blue oceans), freelancers can command higher rates. On the contrary, oversaturated markets (red oceans) may lead to intense competition and downward pressure on pricing.

Creative freelancers should **monitor the balance** between supply and demand in their niche. This involves keeping an eye on industry trends, understanding client needs, and continually refining their skills to meet evolving demands.

How AI Affects Supply And Demand

Since we're talking about the universal principles of supply and demand, this would be a good time to address the "elephant in the room" of what's going on with the explosive technology that's right at our doorstep: **AI**, otherwise known as **Artificial Intelligence**, or **Machine Learning**.

The world we live in is marked by rapid change… and nowhere is that more apparent than the technology that we use - and are surrounded by - every day. While this gives us amazing tools as creatives, it also seems to threaten our very existence! How can we compete in a world where just anybody can type in a simple prompt into an A.I. tool and get a perfectly rendered illustration, written article, or even a video within seconds? Should we just give up now and change careers?

I can certainly understand the fear that this incredible technology may bring. If it helps, our creative industry isn't the only one affected… they *all* are to some degree. **It's my opinion, however, that being a highly capable creative person in a creative industry is SAFER than being in most non-creative industries!**

This is because the work that we do is **intellectual** and **aesthetic**. Creative work done by people carries with it a certain **genuine humanity** that is missing with AI. And, even if someone **can't** tell whether something is generated by a human or an AI tool, many times they still want to know if it was.

The proliferation of "AI-slop" is, in fact, already causing a cultural backlash. There will be an increased desire for **authenticity** and a movement toward **genuine human creative effort.** The laws of supply and demand that influence economics and consumer behavior at all levels will still apply… and that means that YOUR creative ideas and labors, which will be in a limited supply in the coming age, will be ever-increasingly scarce and valuable.

Another thing to keep in mind is that the *true* solution probably isn't going to be "all machine" or "all human"… but rather, a **hybrid of the two**. Many of the tools we use will be AI tools, but we will still be the creatives at the "helm" of the tool. Our creative decision making processes, such as our eye for what looks good and our curation abilities, make us leaders and tastemakers. **People will need other people they can trust to tell them if what the machines are giving them actually looks good.**

And that's the essence of a successful positioning strategy. In order to be a creative in a non-commodity niche, which is what I'm teaching you to do in choosing your niche effectively, is to strive to be a **leader** and a **tastemaker**... **someone who knows how to solve creative problems**... NOT someone who just "pushes the button and gets a prize." When you strive for this, you will always be in the group of elite creative pros who aren't displaced by the machines... instead, you use THEM – and whatever other tool is needed – to help you achieve your creative goals.

How To "AI–Proof" Your Freelance Business

So what does this mean for your freelancing business? Well, if you haven't yet experimented with the AI tools that are out there, **I would recommend that you do.** Many of them offer a free tier to start. Take advantage of that, and try out as many as you can. Experiment, see how they work. You'll soon learn that the results are often quite remarkable, but that one essential thing is missing: *fine control.* You have to relinquish a degree of control to the machine in exchange for the use of its mystical, mysterious technology.

Bingo! You've found your uniqueness, and your creative competitive advantage. Expert control is what YOU offer as a real human: **control** over your medium and your result. We all know clients can be really picky about what they want. They like to be able tweak things. I know that can be annoying, but… **what if that is the thing that actually makes you the most valuable to them?**

Believe it or not, those clients who are playing with AI this very moment are experiencing that same frustration with lack of control. Many of them take their results to a freelancer to fix (I have definitely noticed a lot more of my creative freelance tasks lately involve me having to fix an asset created by a client with AI).

Clients know that the promise of AI tools is to be able to do more with less money. Are they willing to sacrifice control for that? To some degree. But the BEST solution for them (and in general) is to use each tool for what it's best suited for. So they might do some stuff with AI but at the end of the day the higher end projects will always need to go through the hands of a capable creative pro who knows how stuff should look, who can fix the errors, and who can bring it all together into a coherent whole.

And guess what? That creative pro can be YOU.

We're all living on the bleeding edge of the technology here, and stuff changes so often that it takes pretty much daily upkeep on what's going on out there with A.I. – so make a point to stay on top of it. You'll find that it doesn't take much effort to maintain that knowledge once you get over the initial learning curve of what these AI tools even are, but once you get into it, you'll see that many of them essentially work the same way.

The Mindset You Need To Thrive In An AI World

Probably the most important aspect of how this brave new A.I. world affects our creative freelance business is **our mindset about it.** As with any new development that affects your business, accept the change, and slow down and take it one step at a time. The halls of creative history are littered with failed creatives who declared, *"There's no way I'm learning how to do* *<u>that</u>*!"

Sure, AI is the shiny new "belle of the ball" right now, but take a look through time. In the early 90's, when I first got started professionally, and when graphic designers were still creating graphics by hand, **Apple Mac computers** were the brand new interloper in the creative space. This was a time that was known as the "desktop publishing revolution". Many established artists thought laying out graphics on a Mac and printing them out was "cheating" and so many of them rejected it. But the Macs eventually won out – and those old-guard graphic designers who had spent hours trying to draw and cut perfect lines with rulers and X-Acto knives had to get on board or get left behind.

Going all the way back to the printing press, the loom, the industrial revolution… the historical relationship between technology and creative fields is an interesting rabbit hole to explore. Were jobs displaced? Sure. Were tears shed? Absolutely. But those who came out on top were **the ones who took the initiative to learn the new technology and to embrace it.** They found a way to strike a balance between the tried-and-true ways of old and the novel possibilities offered by the new tools.

Look for similarities in these events to the modern times we find ourselves in. You'll often see a pattern: the technology inevitably wins out, but it's not an absolute takeover… it's a **hybrid** between how things were done before, with an incorporation of the new technology. Rather than the "old" or the "new" winning the entire game, it ends up as a "draw" where the result is a blend of both.

And that's how I see the current developments in AI panning out: it won't displace ALL the jobs people are currently in, but it will **enhance** the jobs that people are already doing. Sure, the efficiency increase will mean that while a certain client might have had five designers on staff to do a particular creative task, now they might need only two or even one. However, there are other companies (the smart ones) who will use the tremendous productivity boost to their advantage… and figure out how to use the *same* amount of designers to **increase their overall creative output** with AI, generating more revenue for their company.

One more note I'd like to add: there's often a "**whiplash effect**" with popular new trends and technologies. The faster the adoption, the bigger the resulting backlash is to it. For example, in the aforementioned "desktop publishing revolution", I remember (and some of you might as well) the proliferation of CD-Roms with tens of thousands of clip art files on them. Pretty much overnight, we began to see the most horrendous offenses of design ever perpetuated on the eyes of the public! Flyers began to appear everywhere with an awful mishmash of clashing fonts and artwork. It an explosion of bad taste never before seen.

The result? Thankfully, people *with* taste eventually came to their senses and realized that good design is timeless… and a good designer is still worth paying to do a creative job that needs to be done right. (That said, bad taste does still rear its head at times when an aesthetically-challenged client gets their hands on the latest AI tool after a couple glasses of wine…)

So we've said a lot here about the advent of A.I. and Machine Learning and how it affects your freelance business, and how you can position yourself to benefit from this new technology instead of be displaced by it. I think it's worth **summarizing a few points:**

- Emphasize your **humanity**, your personality, anything that makes you human, areas where AI can't compete.
- Instead of burying your head in the sand about AI, **learn** about these new tools and consider how you can incorporate them to make what you do more efficient.
- Maintain a healthy **mindset** about this new tech, and be ready to offer your clients creative solutions.

Remember, AI is essentially just like any other new tool… it can be resisted, ***or*** it can be learned about and adapted to fit your creative business. The more you're able to speak with authority on these new tools, the more likely your clients will be to see you as a **thought leader, a problem-solver, and an authority** in your field.

Designing Your Positioning Strategy

So far in this part of the book, we've talked a lot of "theory" on market positioning. While I've given you an example of my own particular niche, you might be feeling a little lost, wondering, *"how do I fit into all of this?"* How do you go about understanding your own positioning in the marketplace, your own creative freelance niche?

If you've already been freelancing for awhile, you probably already have a pretty firm idea of where your market and niche are… but you might be open to the possibility of expanding yourself out into some of those overlapping markets where there might be some more opportunity. Maybe you can find a way to edge out into more "blue ocean" waters, to get more specific about what you offer to a more unique client.

If you're fairly new to freelancing, or trying to still determine where your value lies in the market, then this is a good time for you to **figure out where you want to be**. You could benefit from a lot more research in the areas you're interested in, and where you see your skills and talents could be put to good use. You could choose a more "blue ocean" niche right off the bat, targeting your skill acquisition and client attraction efforts in an area where not a lot of freelancers are yet, and shortcut your success.

Wherever you fall in this spectrum of freelancers, one thing is certain: **you need a solid positioning strategy**. If you want to be successful, and become attractive to a select group of ideal clients, it's not enough to just choose a niche and start telling everybody you're available… you need a solid plan on who you want to attract, the kind of work you want to be able to provide them, and how you will go about "magnetizing" your offer.

The Best Positioning Strategy: A "Client-First" Approach

To properly develop your positioning strategy, I believe **the best way to start is with a "client-first" approach.** This works better than a "freelancer-first" approach if you want to become attractive. Rather than try to force-feed your creative offering to your clients, it's better to start with the clients' needs FIRST… and then adjust your offering to meet their needs.

In order to have a "client-first" approach, you need to first be able to **accurately describe** your ideal clients in every way… to completely understand their needs and what they're looking for. You need to get inside their heads, to know what they're thinking.

"Whoa, Mike, this sounds really extreme! How in the world can I possibly know what a client is thinking? That seems excessive, not to mention impossible… "

I'll tell you exactly how you can know what your clients are thinking… because they are all thinking pretty much the same things! They ARE human, like us, after all - and they have roles and responsibilities within their companies that motivate their behaviors. Along with these expectations come beliefs that they have about you and about the work that you do.

Next I'll show you a model that describes the different belief stages that your clients go through as they progress in their knowledge of you and what you do, and how you can help them achieve their goals within their company. When you understand this, and apply it to your freelancing business, you'll gain a powerful tool that informs how you go about attracting the best clients.

The Client Belief Pyramid

The model that we'll talk about to describe your clients' beliefs - and how that affects you getting hired for the job - is called **The Client Belief Pyramid.** (Yes, it's another pyramid... what can I say? I just like pyramids! Pyramids are cool!)

This model answers the all-important questions about what your clients are thinking about their needs, about you, and about how you can possibly help them meet their needs. It also allows you to understand where your clients are in their decision making process about you, and it even gives you insight on how to "guide" your clients down a path that the best decision for their needs is *YOU*... and your creative abilities.

Their journey to hiring (or not hiring) you starts at the bottom of the pyramid and traverses upward, through the different levels. Let's talk about that journey, and **what's going through their minds at each stage.**

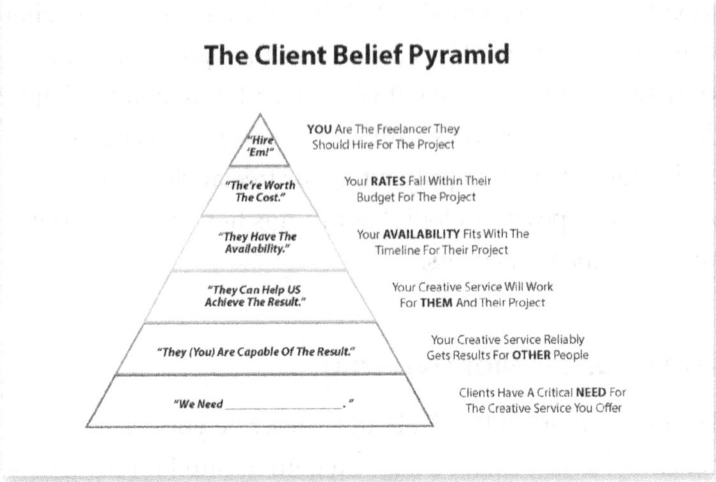

*For a downloadable full-color illustration of the Client Belief Pyramid, visit your bonuses page available at **www.theclientmagnetmethod.com.***

Client Belief #1: They Have A Critical NEED For The Creative Service You Offer.

At the bottom of the pyramid, you don't even enter into the equation yet. **It starts with a NEED.** The clients become **aware** that they have a need for the particular creative service you offer.

This need might arise from a new external job opportunity for them, an internal need, and the lack of an internal employee that has the creative skillset they require. They **form the belief that they must hire a freelancer** to meet this need. (And, depending on the timeline of a particular project or deadline, this need might even be extremely urgent.)

Client Belief #2: They Believe That Your Creative Service Reliably Gets Results For OTHER People.

As a client begins their search for freelancer to meet their needs, they come across **you**. They might see your body of work displayed online, or perhaps it's shown to them by an internal employee, a word of mouth referral inside or outside the company, or by a recruiter. They look at this and your other Authority Factors and form the belief that **you are able to reliably get results for other people.**

Client Belief #3: They Believe That Your Creative Service Can Work For THEM And Their Project Or Situation.

After clients see that you can get results for others, they **reflect** on *their* particular situation and **compare** their situation with the situation of the clients you've achieved results for. If they feel there is a big difference between the two, then they might have **objections** that would need to be overcome before hiring you.

Remember our earlier example way back in the chapter on competence, when we talked about purple dinosaurs vs. yellow dinosaurs? This is where I've seen a lot of possible jobs fall through, because a client might for example need a video of a purple dinosaur. They see that you've made a video of a *yellow* dinosaur for another client. *"Hmm,"* they ask themselves, *"I see they can do yellow dinosaurs… but can they do* purple *ones, which is what we need?"* Sure, this sounds silly… but I can't tell you how many times clients have gotten hung up on stuff like this!

Clients can often get very literal. They want close to 100 percent certainty that you will be able to help them achieve their result. This becomes more complicated when there are layers of approvals involved, and people downshift into "fear" mode, where preserving their job becomes a priority. You might not even see or become aware of these factors, but just know that if you do see weird questions from a client, then these may the kinds of things at play here.

From the outside, you're just seeing the "tip of the iceberg" compared to what your clients see. So, as the outside freelancer, just know that this is where you are in the process of the Client Belief Pyramid… and have an **extra measure of patience.** Be prepared to explain how it's not a problem for you to give them "purple dinosaurs." With your patience and willingness to overcome any objections - and well as your awareness about what's probably going on behind the scenes - you'll be able to get though this client belief stage and on to the next.

One more thing to say here… these first three stages **might even occur before you are even aware of them!** A client may discover their need, find you online, look at your Authority Factors, and come to the conclusion you are the person for their job… all on their own! It's happened to me quite a bit, actually. If your Authority Factors are convincing enough, then the very first contact a client has with you might be all the way to these next stages, price and availability. (Now, doesn't that sound easy?)

Client Belief #4: They Believe That Your AVAILABILITY Fits With The Timeline Of The Project.

After client belief number three, it's all downhill from there… since they're already decided you can help them, from that point onward it's all about logistics. (Assuming the job doesn't fall through at the last minute!) **Availability** concerns the **timeline they have for their project, and the time you have available to help them when they need it.**

This is when you both whip the calendars out. There might be some need for you to be flexible here, because the client might not have a firm timeline set in stone. You, as a freelancer, are likely more flexible than they are, so this is when you will want to be diligent with your schedule and be certain that you will be able to accommodate their timeframe, as well as account for any possible variations in their schedule.

The good news is, **they've already decided** that you can help them achieve the result they need, so you're on the "inside track" here.

Client Belief #5: They Believe That Your RATES Fall Within Their Budget For The Project.

It's possible that **discussion of rates** has already happened before this… but it needs to be put somewhere, and it very likely could occur here, especially if they already have an idea of the budget they have to work with, and a preconceived idea of what your rates are. You would quote your rates, whether they be hourly, day rates, or a fixed rate for the entire job, along with any exceptions, such as overtime or any other fees.

If this is the stage when rates first get discussed – since you're on the "inside track" at this stage, and you know they already want to work with you, there is some negotiating power here. This is also where the scheduling talk might merge into the rate discussion. For example, if the project has a very tight time frame, there might be weekend work or overtime involved, and your rates will need to flex accordingly. (I charge 1.5 times my day rate for overtime and weekend work, which is pretty standard for my particular market, so I would bring this up at this point.)

Client Belief #6: YOU Are The Freelancer They Should Hire For The Project.

This is the last belief, where your client has already overcome all the possible barriers and objections to hiring you, and all systems are go! **They believe you are the freelancer to hire for this task.**

In other words, to quote a popular cultural phrase, your clients are saying at this point: *"Shut up and take my money!"*

Now their goal is to get your locked down on the project as soon as possible. At that point it's just about the formalities of getting you onboarded to their project, filling out papers, NDA's, etc. Congratulations! You have the gig.

Now that we've covered the Client Belief Pyramid, you're equipped with a great sense of the processes… as well as the **beliefs**… that clients go though during their decision-making process to hire you. Does that feel a bit more empowering now? Since you've actually crawled inside your clients' heads (eew) now you likely understand them a bit better. (Maybe it even makes you feel a bit less frustrated when you *don't* get the gig, considering all the stuff they have to think about!)

We've learned a bit about what makes our clients tick… the next step is to dig a bit deeper into WHO your clients are. And for that, you need a "Field Guide".

Creative Clients: A Field Guide

My grandmother, who we affectionately called Ninny, was no "ninny" when it came to knowing things. Especially when it came to **birds**.

She and my grandfather had some land in rural Texas, and different varieties of birds would frequent their property. As a kid, I commented one day on how much she seemed to know about the different birds, their variations, their calls, and even their habits. With a wink, she went into the house and pulled out a colorful book called *A Field Guide To The Birds Of Texas*.

There they were, illustrated in full color: all the birds we were seeing around the property. There was also a lot of info about birds that we didn't see around their land, but we *could* see if we got in the car and started driving around the state looking for them. (Which she did as well from time to time, I learned!)

If you want to be successful as a freelancer - to be seen as an authority in your field, and to be compensated accordingly - then you'll need a **field guide**. You'll want to know where the best clients hang out, how to recognize them, and how to attract them. You'll want to know what motivates them, what makes them tick, what causes them to act the way they do.

You'll need to learn what they value, what frustrates them, and what keeps them up at night.

Now, wouldn't it be great if such a field guide existed? Well, here's a bit of good news: **we can make one together!** In the following pages I'll walk you through the steps to make your very own Client Field Guide that's customized just for you.

Not only that, I've also provided a **Client Field Guide Workbook** that you can fill out as we go along. It lives here along with your other book bonuses:

TheClientMagnetMethod.com

This will be an interactive exercise… so get ready to roll up those sleeves! Fortunately, the research that I'll guide you through is mostly online, so you can do it from the comfort of your couch. While wearing pajamas, if you wish. (Hey, you do you!)

Not All Clients Are Created Equal

The clients who might pay for your creative services are **not all the same**. Even within the same market, they might behave differently, have different pay rates, and different motivations within their company. Furthermore, depending on how "deep" you go into an organization, there are "layers" of people that you need to understand, especially the larger the organization is.

If you're already an experienced freelancer with clients, perhaps you'd like *better* clients, or want to investigate other *markets* with possibly better clients. If so, you're in the right place! Go into this with an open mind and re-examine your client roster and the work you do. The upcoming exercise will help you do that.

Building Your Client "Avatar"

Assuming you already have an idea of the creative work that you'd like to do, then we need to find the ***ideal*** clients who are interested in that work. There might be a number of places you can look. Perhaps you have some obvious ones in mind, based on your experience… or maybe at this point you still don't have *any* clients, and that's okay too, you can use your imagination for now!

It starts with an accurate **vision** of who your PERFECT client is. (Hey, you're creative, so you should be really great at this vision stuff!) This ideation of your perfect client is also known as your **client avatar**.

No, you don't have to envision your clients as overly tall blue-tinted people who live on another planet. An **avatar** is a **detailed, fictional profile representing your ideal client, based on data and research.** Having a crystal clear idea of your avatar is *essential* to getting the clients you really want, because it allows you to deeply understand them, the goals, their ideals, and their motivations. With this clarity, you'll be able to search and locate them much more effectively.

A point of clarification: while you might have a number of different people you interact with at a company that hires you to do work, the avatar we're envisioning is the actual person

who makes the decision to hire you. While these might not be the same people you work with day-to-day on a job, they are the most critical people to focus on locating and attracting as clients.

The Client Compass

The *Client Compass* is a good framework for thinking about what really motivates your clients and what makes them "tick". It examines your client's Goals, Pains, Fears and Values (also Beliefs.)

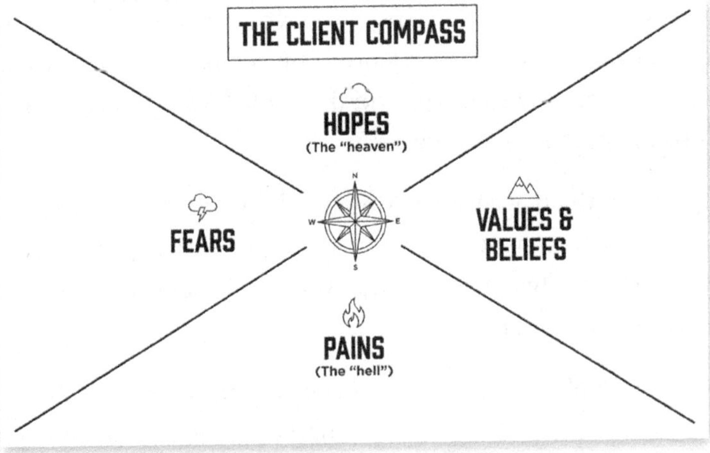

Here are some questions that are worth identifying about your ideal client's "compass", along with some sub-prompts to get you going. This is really a brainstorming session, so there are no wrong answers. Write out your thoughts, going with the **first thing** that pops into your head:

1. What are your avatar's <u>goals?</u> (The "heaven")

- *What's their objective at their company, what are they tasked to do?*
- *What do they ultimately want out of their career?*
- *What status do they want to achieve?*
- *What are they hoping to accomplish by hiring someone like you?*
- *How will they measure their success?*
- *What makes them look like a "hero" to their peers?*
- *What kind of emotion are they looking forward to when you come through for them?*

2. What are your avatar's pains? (the "hell")

- *What are the biggest challenges that they regularly face?*
- *What negative feelings and emotions are they trying to avoid?*
- *What is the "clog" that is slowing them down?*
- *What problem is causing them to lose money?*
- *What makes them sigh with frustration every day?*
- *What have they tried and failed at? Who are they afraid of disappointing the most?*

3. What are your avatar's fears?

- *Are they more afraid of losing money, time, or their reputation?*
- *Why might they think you won't be able to help them?*
- *What objections might they have to hiring you?*
- *What is their 'nightmare scenario' that wakes them up at 3 a.m.?*
- *Who are they afraid of disappointing if the project doesn't go well?*
- *What's the ONE feeling they're trying the most to avoid?*

4. What are your avatar's values & beliefs?

- *What's most important to them? What do they deeply care about?*
- *What are their core beliefs?*
- *What brands, products, or other things do they feel proud to be associated with?*
- *What's more important to them: freedom or security? Innovation or tradition? Speed or quality? Logic or emotion?*
- *What is the one thing they would never want someone to say about them? (e.g., that they are 'cheap,' 'unreliable,' or 'unoriginal'). Who is their role model?*

Now, up until I threw out this list of crazy questions, you might not have ever thought about your clients in this way. Your answer for an ideal client might have been, *"one that actually pays me!"*

When we set the bar (and our expectations) low and vague, then we tend to look for and *expect* that standard. We might begin to think that we're unable to find clients whose quality level is barely above the level of "they pay something." This can cause us to settle for **less** than we actually deserve. And, yes, my fellow freelancer friend, **you DO deserve great clients.** You've worked hard to get where you are, you've spent many hours honing your craft. YES… **you deserve great clients!**

In fact, I want you to tell yourself that right now. No matter where you are, no matter if your partner or pet or coworker looks at you funny, I want you to tell yourself out loud: ***"I deserve great clients!"***

Now, with that little pep talk over with, let's examine our list, shall we? Maybe it looks like a pipe dream. Maybe that picture-perfect client looks a lot like yourself... that's to be expected! There's nothing wrong with wanting to work with people we identify with.

Let's distill our 'compass' with the four main categories of questions into a succinct, clear picture of who our client is. Fill in the blanks of the following sentence:

"My Ideal Client is a [Job Title/Role] who feels [Current Pain] and is looking for [Ultimate Gain], but they are secretly worried that [Greatest Fear]. They value [Core Belief] above all else."

We're really getting to know this person now, aren't we?

Let's top off our avatar's profile by filling out the following information about your avatar:

- Name
- Age
- Gender
- Marital Status
- Number and Age of Children
- Location
- Level of Education
- Other

While this might *seem* unnecessary, it's very important because it helps you personify this "ideal client". Sure, you probably won't find a client *exactly* like this (that would be really spooky, right?) but even if you get anywhere close, you're in the neighborhood.

The most important thing this does is that it gives you that image in your mind of a real person that you really want to work with. This helps *you* tremendously as you send your work out in to the dark void of cyberspace because you can imagine you're not just communicating with an anonymous entity – you're reaching out to your avatar, who you've imagined as a real person. Doesn't that sound more fun?

Client Research

Now that we've created an "ideal standard" for the kinds of clients we want to work for (the "compass"), it's time to do our **research** (the "map") so that we can go and **find** them.

This is where our ideals meet reality. I'm going to state the obvious here: you aren't going to find that perfect client right off the bat! You might find clients that fit *some* or even *most* of the criteria, though. And that's totally okay… because regardless of how close we get to that ideal, **we've still raised the standard for ourselves.**

This part involves going online into the untamed wilderness of the internet and doing some client-hunting. The easiest places to look for clients online is through Google search and LinkedIn. We'll talk more about LinkedIn in our next section on Chapter 4 - Platform, but for now we'll use it as our primary research tool.

You might have a list of companies (or the kinds of companies) that you would like to freelance for. **Do a search** for each of those companies on Google and LinkedIn now.

Using Google, **find the company's website.** Then look for an About page, or Company page, that hopefully lists people at the company. For smaller, privately owned companies and studios, you might find a list of people and their job titles, but for a larger company, you may not. That's okay, that's where our next part of the search comes in.

Next, using LinkedIn, do a search for the same company, and click "**View Page**" to see the company's LinkedIn profile page. Then click on the link at the top of their page that says "**People**". We've struck a gold mine! This will show a much more complete list of the people who actually work at the company. It even shows bar charts of where in the world they live, where they studied, their job titles and what they're skilled at. Under that, if you're already active on LinkedIn, you could even see people you may know as first and second degree connections.

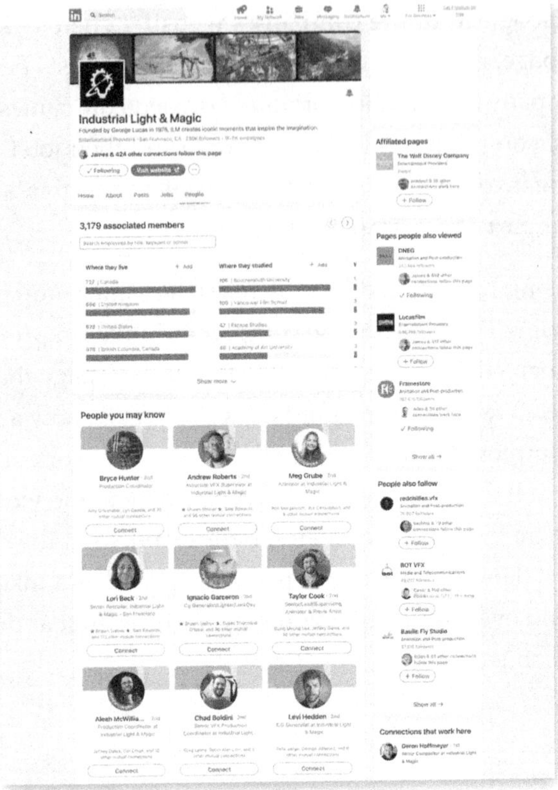

The robust "People" tab of a LinkedIn company page

As you scroll further down the page, you'll see the different people on LinkedIn who work for the company, along with their job titles. As you scroll even further down, it lists people who don't necessarily work at the company but who are freelancers or have been associated with the company in the past. Here's where you will want to take note of the people who could be potential coworkers and clients, and consider connecting with them.

The right column of the page (if viewing on a desktop) yields even more information, such as affiliated pages and companies, and other connections you might have who also work at the company. These provide great jumping-off points for further research, and for finding out companies that you might not even know about. The "rabbit-hole" of all the possible clients and companies out there might be vast and overwhelming… but when you think about it, isn't that a great "problem" to have?

Outer vs. Inner Layer Clients

Here's where it helps to discern the different kids of people who work at a company… because not everybody will be potential client contacts.

The ones you will be looking at primarily will be the ones whose job it is to find people like YOU. In larger companies, these might be people with titles like HR Manager, Director Of Operations, Staffing Supervisor, etc. This is what I call "**Outer Layer**" client contacts. These people are typically the **first point of contact** between freelancers and the people that the freelancers will actually be working with.

One thing to keep in mind… it might not be as cut and dried as you might think… the people hiring for a particular company might not even technically work *at* the company. This includes people like "headhunters" and recruiters who get a little kickback from a company for finding people. I've gotten a couple of jobs this way over the years, and it's great because it can "shortcut" the process of getting hired on a job. These Outer Layer contacts can be very key people to get to know as well.

"Inner layer" client contacts are people who are further in the company… and includes the folks you would actually be working with day to day on a job. These people are split between supervisor types, like project managers, producers, or executive producers, and worker-bee types, like the people who would be on your level, with titles similar to your own… these could even be other freelancers who do what you do. **The outer layer people often hand freelancers off to the inner layer people.**

Again, there is a big distinction between large and smaller companies here. For smaller companies the "outer layer" and the "inner layer" might be the same person! For larger organizations, there might be several layers of people.

It's important to distinguish between all these different kinds of clients, because while they all work for the same company, they have different goals and objectives. They also may have very different personalities and ways of dealing with people.

But you don't know any of this right now… for now, all you know is what the person does and the company they work for. (Although, you can click on their name and look at their posts to find out more.) For now, **begin making a list of all of the Outer Layer clients you can find.**

If you wish, you can list Inner Layer ones as well… but for this exercise, since the Outer Layer ones are key to getting you hired, let's find them first, and you can always come back to the Inner Layer ones later.

A List Of Possible "Outer Layer" Job Titles

To help you in your search for Outer Layer clients, and to give you a jumping-off point of what kinds of job titles to look for, here is a sample list. This list is by no means comprehensive, and as I mentioned earlier, it can vary depending on the company and market you're in.

- HR Recruiting Specialist
- HR Recruiter
- HR Manager
- HR Generalist
- HR Representative
- HR Specialist
- Human Resources
- Human Resources Officer
- Recruiter
- Recruiting Specialist
- Recruiting Lead
- Recruiting Coordinator
- Recruiting Manager
- Recruitment Manager
- Head Of Recruiting
- External Recruiter
- Director Of Recruiting
- Recruiting Leader
- Technical Recruiter
- Lead Recruiter
- Senior Recruiter
- Principal Recruiter
- Trade Recruiter
- Field Recruiter
- Recruiting Coordinator
- Recruiting & Onboarding
- Associate Recruiter
- Recruitment & Talent Specialist
- Talent Acquisition Specialist
- Talent Acquisition Recruiter
- Talent Acquisition Manager
- Talent Acquisition Lead
- Director Of Talent Acquisition

- Talent Lead
- Talent Recruiter
- Talent Manager
- Talent Specialist
- Talent Partner
- Talent Coordinator
- Talent / Recruitment
- Head Of Talent
- Staffing
- Staffing Specialist
- Staffing Recruiter
- Staffing Coordinator
- Staffing Manager
- Artist Manager
- Creative Hiring
- Lead Of Creative Hiring
- Creative Recruiter
- Creative Staffing Specialist
- Creative Talent Specialist
- Creative Talent Recruiter
- Freelance Recruiter
- Freelance Talent Specialist
- Head Of Artistic Recruiting

Inside-Out vs. Outside-In

Another reason it's important to categorize the different clients you might be dealing with is that **the Outer Layer of clients will be the ones whose job it is to find and hire people like you.** They'll be paying attention to freelancer profiles with job descriptions like yours. So it makes sense that these are the potential clients who you will want to be attractive to. We could call this the **"Outside-In" approach.**

There's another way to get work… the **"Inside Out" approach.** This would be when a person from the Inner Layer of clients – a manager or supervisor at that company, or even a worker-level person – recommends you. This is more rare because these people have jobs to do, and they aren't looking around for you like the Outer Layer people are. They also usually have a limited capacity to choose the kind of people they get to work with. (However, as you complete successful freelance jobs and get "in" with these people, they will be more likely to recommend you and ask for you in the future!)

So keep your mind open to both possibilities, both Inside-Out and Outside-In… but in general, when you're looking for new work with new clients, the **Outside-In method is much more effective… and also more common.**

Completing Your Client Field Guide

As you do your homework, looking at companies and finding the different layers of potential clients, fill out your "field guide". This research might take awhile, but it's well worth it! It will not only give you a list of people to potentially reach out to, but it will also give you a good sense of the market you're looking at working with.

You might even decide to use a piece of software called a **CRM** (which stands for Customer Relationship Management) to catalog your different potential clients. This can be a very valuable tool, because you can use it to update your contacts, and manage and track your conversations with them. There are a lot of CRM's out there to choose from. I like **HubSpot (www.hubspot.com)** because it's powerful, easy to use, and it's free.

Ideally, you're never quite "finished" with your client field guide… it should be something that you keep updating as your clients (and the companies they work for) shift and move around. The good news is, if you've taken the time to create it in the first place, you've done the heavy lifting, and it should be easy to maintain it from there with a little bit of effort.

A Bonus LinkedIn "Power Tip"

Here's a great little "power tip" that has helped me in the past to identify possible clients.

One cool feature of LinkedIn is that it will sometimes send you an email that looks like this:

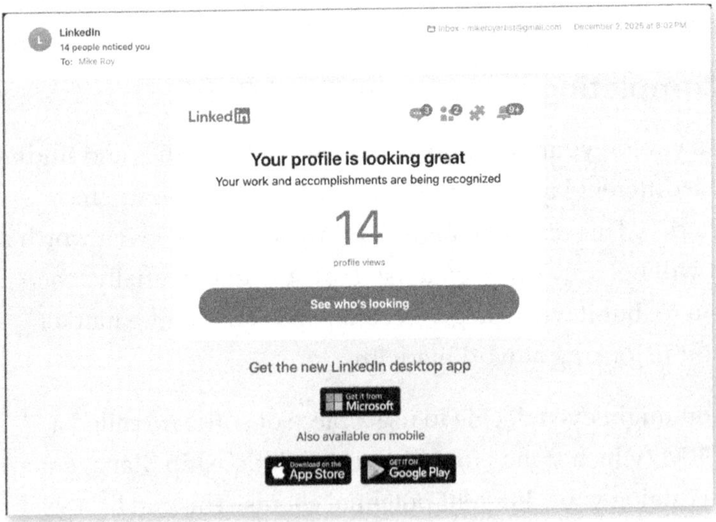

Now, how cool is this?! It's like a "tripwire" around your digital property that lets you know when a prospective client has been sniffing around your territory! When you click the

"See who's looking" button, you'll come across something like this:

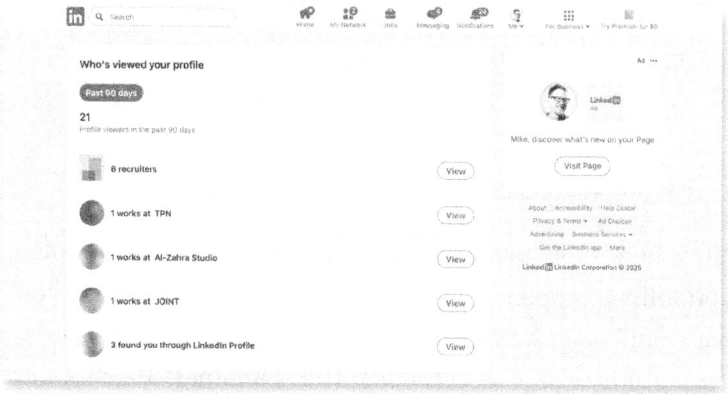

This is even more valuable "intel" that can tell you the sorts of folks who have been interested in looking at your services. (In your quest to become magnetic, LinkedIn has already done some of the work for you – these people already know about you and are curious about what you offer!)

Notice that the information is a bit vague, and only points to their company, not the actual person who has been looking for you. This is an "upsell" feature of LinkedIn and apparently if you subscribe to LinkedIn Premium you can actually see the people (currently they offer one month free to try it out). But in my case, since many of the companies I've worked with are smaller studios, I've never really felt the need to upgrade this, because I then go to the company page and check it out.

When I do, it's usually pretty obvious which subset of folks have been peeking into my world. And it doesn't really matter because… if they seem like a company I'd like to work with, then I'll go ahead and send invites to connect with *all* of them. Many times I'll send a little message along with the connection request along the lines of this:

> *"Hi there, it looks like we run in the same circles professionally, so I thought we might connect here on LinkedIn. Have a great day! – Mike."*

See? Not too hard. Simple.

Now, here's the powerful bit… what if one of those people you follow happens to be the very person who checked your page out? *What a coincidence,* they might think, *I was just looking at their page the other day.* That's another "touchpoint" where a prospective client can see your name and anchor your authority in their mind… and it's super-easy to do. Thanks, LinkedIn! (Now are you starting to see why I like this platform so much?)

Positioning Yourself For Success

Let's review what we talked about in this chapter on Positioning.

Positioning is a very important component of the Client Magnet Method because it allows you to **place yourself** - and your creative freelance services - in the **best possible light to attract your ideal clients.**

Positioning yourself as a professional service provider in the creative freelance marketplace is an art that requires a blend of **skill, strategy**, and **adaptability**. By embracing specificity, adapting your strategy, and understanding the economic landscape of your niche, freelancers can not only attract the right clients but also command top pay rates.

When you're in the right market, you're swimming in "**blue**" and "**purple**" oceans where your services are **more tailored, unique, and valuable to your clients.** This allows you to avoid "red ocean" freelancer markets where competition is fierce and pay is low.

In a world where differentiation is key, creative freelancers must navigate the waters they swim in with purpose. Choose your part of the ocean carefully, and you'll have the kind of ideal business that rewards you with the ideal clients - and income - that you want. I used my own field as an example of how a freelancer might position themselves to take advantage of adjacent markets, with different clients, while using the same skillset.

We discussed the advent of **AI and Machine Learning tools** and how they have affected the freelance landscape, and how they might affect your positioning. We talked about ways you can adapt your freelance business to **take advantage of them**, rather than be disrupted by them.

A **"client-first" strategy** is ideal for establishing your market, and it starts with understanding the **thought process** - and **beliefs** – about you and your work that clients undergo before making the decision to hire you. Knowing this process can empower you to help them come to the conclusion that you're the best freelancer for the job.

Next, we talked about formulating in your mind **your ideal of a "perfect client"**… the ones who value you and who you would love to work with. With this ideal in mind, you can begin to craft your **"Client Field Guide"** and do the necessary research on Google and LinkedIn to locate and catalog the different clients who will be ideal points of contact.

From this research, you will be able to target the **"Outer Layer" clients**, who are looking for freelancers just like you. You'll also understand the "Inner Layer" clients who are the ones inside the company that you would be working with more directly. Primarily, you would use the **"Outside-In" strategy** to make sure you're attractive to the Outer Layer clients, who are the keys to getting hired at your ideal companies.

Once you've gotten to know these clients, and successfully done jobs with them, you'll have a great sense of the clients you love working with ... and chances are, they'll love working with you, too, and they will **recommend and ask for you in the future.** As your freelancing business grows and matures, you'll reap the abundant benefits from becoming a go-to authority in your space.

CHAPTER 4
PLATFORM

Wanna Get Noticed? Choose The Right Platform.

The next key to becoming a magnetic freelancer is the PLATFORM (or platforms) you use to get yourself noticed by clients.

These days, there are a LOT of platforms that exist where a freelancer can market themselves. In fact, one might say there are TOO many! A basic search reveals an overwhelming amount of places where you can spend time learning how to navigate them, building a reputation, and maintaining your presence. Where would you even begin?

Here's a list of the different kinds of options out there, separated into categories. (Chances are, if you've been freelancing awhile, you're already using one or more of them.) We'll talk about their effectiveness in attracting clients. Lastly, I'll share my recommendation of the main platform you should be spending the majority of your time using… because it actually **works**.

A List Of Platforms Freelancers Can Use

Freelance Platforms

These platforms are specifically geared toward matching people with jobs with freelancers who can do those jobs. Some are very broad and others are more niche-specific.

- Upwork
- Freelancer
- Fiverr
- Guru
- Toptal
- Robert Half
- SimplyHired
- 99Designs

Portfolio Websites

These platforms offer a way for freelancers to host their own gallery or portfolio or body of work online.

- Behance
- DeviantArt
- ArtStation
- GitHub (for developers)
- Krop

Social Media Platforms

These platforms are widely used by a lot of people, not just freelancers, but can be used by freelancers to connect with potential clients and peers, and to show work.

- Facebook
- Instagram
- LinkedIn
- X (formerly Twitter)
- Pinterest
- TikTok

Creative Networking Events

These are events hosted either on various online platforms or in real life where you can network with peers and potential clients.

- Industry Conferences
- Seminars
- Webinars
- Meetups
- Workshops
- Exhibitions

Online Forums And Job Boards

These are online forums that target specific niches or broader categories with niches subdivided into specific niches.

- Creative Circle
- Smashing Magazine job board
- AIGA Design Jobs
- Authentic Jobs
- Online Communities
- Reddit (subreddits related to freelancing, design, writing, etc.)
- Creative Cow
- Logik (my own neck of the woods!)
- Dribble's Freelance Project Board and Job Board
- The Design Kids
- We Work Remotely
- Coroflot
- DesignJobsBoard
- If You Could Jobs
- DesignObserver
- Motionographer Jobs

Local Business Chambers and Networking Groups:

These are live, in-person events specifically for businesses to learn and network with one another. This is great for freelancers to find local clients in a specific industry near where they live.

- Chamber of Commerce events
- Local business networking events
- Meetup.com

Collaboration Platforms

These are platforms geared specifically for tech-based freelancers.

- GitHub
- GitLab
- BitBucket

Industry-Specific Websites

These are platforms specializing in a specific industry or collection of industries. Many are full-fledged magazines offering a number of resources, including jobs and the opportunity to be featured in or write articles.

- Mandy Network (for film and TV professionals)
- ProductionHUB (for media production)
- AIGA (American Institute Of Graphic Arts - for Graphic Designers)
- Motionographer (for motion graphic artists)
- Creative Bloq (graphic design, illustration, typography)
- Smashing Magazine (for web designers)
- IMDB (Internet Movie Database)
- Creative Review
- Design Milk - Architecture & Interiors
- My Modern Met
- Dezeen - Architecture & Design
- Ignant - Art, Fashion, Architecture, Design, & Photography
- 500px - Photography

- Abduzeedo
- It's Nice That
- DesignObserver
- British Journal Of Photography
- Aesthetica - Art & Culture
- Sight and Sound - Film
- Campaign - Advertising and Marketing
- The Drum - Marketing, Advertising, Design
- Little Black Book - Advertising
- Ad Age - Advertising
- AdWeek - Advertising, Media
- Wallpaper - Design, Architecture, Art, Fashion
- IDEO - Design, Creative Industry
- DesignWeek
- CartoonBrew - Animation, Film
- Business Of Fashion - Fashion

Content Creation Platforms

These platforms offer an opportunity to write and post articles to establish your knowledge and authority on a variety of relevant topics.

- Medium
- Vocal Media
- Substack
- Patreon

Advertising

This is a pay-to-play game, for sure... but it might just be a great way to get exposure in front of some high-powered clients that wouldn't otherwise know about you. Ad platforms often offer tools to help you target specific people and businesses... and many other freelancers won't be using them.

- Google Ads
- Facebook Ads
- Instagram Ads
- LinkedIn Ads
- newspapers
- magazines
- local mailers

Other Platforms

- Your *own* platform, of course! (Your personal website)
- Create a newsletter and share it with potential clients
- Email outreach to businesses in your niche
- Distribute business cards in local businesses
- University and College Job Boards
- Podcasts: Your own or guest appearances on podcasts related to your field

Whew! Overwhelmed yet?

This list is by no means comprehensive. You may also find additional industry-specific platforms as you zero in on your specific creative niche... which is actually a much better quality place to go than a more generalized one.

In any case, tackling this list can be a real bear… and I'm not going to even attempt to. That's why I want to give you a tool for evaluating them for yourself. For any of these platforms that look interesting to you (or ones you may have already spent considerable time on), here's what I would challenge you to find answers to:

Four Questions To Answer When Choosing A Platform

1. *What's the quality level of the clients who use this platform?*
2. *How relevant is the platform to your creative niche and to your ideal client?*
3. *Will my prospective client be able to easily find me?*
4. *What time, effort, and money would you have to invest to reach your ideal clients?*

When you put these platforms to the test, and go through the exercise of seeking the answers to these questions, it can be very illuminating.

I would invite you to avoid the hype surrounding certain platforms, and the bias you might have towards others, and **purely look at the answers to these questions.** There's a difference between "being entertained" and being enriched professionally… being aware of this distinction can save you a lot of time by looking in the right places for clients.

A Few Platforms To Re-Evaluate

While I said I wasn't going to talk about every single platform on that list, I will take a moment and talk about a couple of kinds of platforms that I see freelancers using quite a bit... but that are not as effective as they think. Maybe these platforms are great for other stuff, but not necessarily great for getting freelance work.

Social Media

I know that a LOT of creative freelancers like to use **social media platforms** like Instagram. They spend quite a bit of time going through people's posts, posting their own work, and responding to feedback. It's a great platform... it's visual, it's easy to use, and it's really good for scanning and sharing visual content. Maybe you use Instagram, and I'm not saying there's anything wrong with that... you do you, boo!

While social media platforms like TikTok and Instagram may provide visibility within a community... even creative communities... **it does not always translate into visibility to paying clients**. The informal nature of these platforms can attract fellow creatives, enthusiasts, or businesses looking for collaboration rather than professional services.

If you use social media to get freelance clients, I'd like to invite you to ask those four questions I asked above. Sure, maybe you get a lot of response from your followers and your peers... and maybe you even have a large following. But how many actual paying clients has it gotten you?

Please don't be offended if you have spent time building up your profile and followers on Instagram, or any other platform for that matter. All I'm doing is asking you to look at the facts, and to look at the data. If the time you spend actually does get you clients... then that's great! But if not... or you're not getting as many clients as you'd like... then know there's probably a solution out there that offers a more effective use of your time.

Freelancing Platforms

You might be wondering why I'd question using a **freelancing platform**. You might be thinking, "What? Why would a freelancer not use a freelancing platform? Isn't that who it's for?"

These platforms, such as Upwork or Fiverr, seem to offer the goods. Upload your profile, put your info in there, and sit back and wait for the work to flood in.

The problem is... and I'm just being honest... the **quality of the clients** (and freelancers, for that matter) **on these platforms isn't usually very high.** You may find work, sure... it just won't be work that you necessarily will be proud to show off. Or, the clients will expect very low prices.

These platforms also tend to be super-competitive, and you'll find yourself swimming with lots of other freelancers from all around the world who are willing to accept low prices - and that's as red as "red ocean" gets. If you're just starting out and want to just get a few jobs and experience under your belt, then sure, go ahead and give it a try… just don't let those platforms dictate the work and the clients that you get, because there's much better opportunity somewhere else.

The One Platform To Rule Them All

Those four questions can help you in your search for your ideal platform. But for those of you who want to just cut to the chase, to have me just tell you right out the best platform to use (in my humble opinion) then I'll do that now.

For many creative niches, I find that there is **one** platform that stands above all the rest. Maybe I'm biased, because it's the platform that I found most of my clients on… clients that helped me build my freelancing business to over six figures in less than a year. (And that was the very first year I started freelancing!)

That platform is… **LinkedIn**.

Maybe some of you are groaning at this. I can hear the complaints now:

> *"But… it's so 'corporate America'. Yuck!"*
>
> *"But… it's not considered "cool" like the other, newer platforms."*
>
> *"But… it's owned by Microsoft. Double Yuck!"*

I hear you. I had many of those same reservations… until I learned that that's where the BEST CLIENTS are.

LinkedIn: Targeted Professionalism for Paying Clients

Here are some of the advantages of using LinkedIn as your primary platform that you spend time using to attract clients to your creative freelance business:

- **Professional Network**: LinkedIn's primary focus on professionals attracts businesses and individuals seeking high-quality, professional services. Every feature is geared toward connecting people in symbiotic, win-win relationships.
- **Showcasing Work and Qualifications**: Place prominent links to your portfolio, reel, or website… right near the top of your profile page. A dedicated section allows freelancers to effectively highlight skills and achievements, and work experience.
- **Targeted Networking**: Directly connecting with potential clients and then communicating through built-in messaging fosters meaningful conversations and increases the likelihood of securing high-value projects.
- **Industry-Specific Groups**: LinkedIn offers industry-specific groups for discussions, insights sharing, and networking, leading to valuable opportunities.
- **Trust and Credibility**: LinkedIn's professional atmosphere encourages clients to prioritize trust and credibility in their freelancer selection.
- **Robust Job Functionality**: LinkedIn offers a dedicated jobs section, the ability to post and directly apply for jobs, and the ability to search for jobs by

industry and category, as well as whether you're looking for full-time, freelance, remote, or hybrid gigs.

- **Low Signal To Noise Ratio**: LinkedIn's interface is designed to be streamlined for business to business use. That's what your freelancing is… a business. And your business doesn't need your clients becoming distracted by cat gifs, pictures of random food, or the latest conspiracy theories of Uncle Earl.

I know, I know. I sound like a spokesperson or something. But if you aren't on there yet, or you have a login but really haven't done anything with it, then I encourage you spend the time to fill out your profile and reach out to make some connections.

I guarantee you'll be glad you did! LinkedIn's professional context attracts clients seeking skilled freelancers just like you. It bridges the gap between showcasing creativity and presenting yourself as a reliable, professional service provider.

Need some help setting up your LinkedIn profile in the best possible way to attract the clients who are looking for YOU? You're in luck… I have a resource to help you do just that. You can check it out at *theclientmagnetmethod.com*, along with the other bonuses you received by being a member of my distinguished society of readers.

Review: Your Creative Business Needs A Platform!

In this section we talked about platforms, the different places your clients can find out about you. While these are mostly online methods, we talked about a few in-person platforms as well.

Choose your platforms carefully! You might spend a lot of time on a platform, to find out that it's not actually as effective as you thought. Not all platforms are created equal… and while some are easier to use and might seem to be "low hanging fruit" for getting clients, like social media, **they aren't necessarily going to give you the clients you need** to build your freelancing business.

Finally, we spent time discussing my recommendation for a platform that works well for freelancers, which is **LinkedIn**. Since it's focused primarily on business interactions, this keeps it "pure" from the noise that other platforms suffer from. Plus, it's where many of your best clients already are… and they're on there, right now, **looking for freelancers like you** to help them.

Whatever you decide to choose as your platform or platforms, make it a habit to **re-evaluate their effectiveness** compared to the effort they require to use. Your choices … and your efforts…. could pay off with a flood of great clients who will grow your creative freelance business for years to come!

CHAPTER 5
TIMING

Getting In Sync With Your Clients

The next part of the Client Magnet Method that I want to talk about is TIMING.

The better your timing is with a client, the more "in sync" you both are - and therefore the more *magnetic* you will be to them.

What do I mean by being "in sync"? (And how is this even something we can do anything about?)

Let me give you an example from my own experience. There have been moments when I've checked in with a client, or they checked in with me, and things just "seemed to fall into place at the right time". Maybe I contacted them right as they were discussing the need for a freelancer, or they just had a job awarded and they were beginning to think about staffing up for it. It seems to feel like more than just a coincidence, and so our minds seem to give these seemingly chance "coincidences" even more importance.

This is a wonderful, rare thing, and it even has a term: **Synchronicity**. (Which is a principle explored by a psychologist named Carl Jung that also happens to be the name of my favorite album by the band *The Police*… but I digress.)

MUCH more often, though, this DOESN'T happen. Even after you've worked hard to attain authority in the mind of your clients, the timing between our availability and our client's needs seems "off"… and it can be frustrating.

How many times have you reached out to a client (or a client reached out to you) about possible work, and while all the other things seemed to align toward working together, there was one thing in the way: **it just wasn't the right timing?**

Schedules and projects can be a complex puzzle, and you might miss out on netting a great client simply because of "bad timing".

So can we actually do anything about this? You may be surprised when I answer, "*Yes.*" **Because you can!**

How Chance Can Be Manipulated

Here's a little thought exercise for you. My goal is to show you that something we think of as "random luck" … like you and a client having mutual needs at the same time… can be actually manipulated to your advantage.

Let's say I flip a coin… heads, you win, tails, I win. So you have a 50 percent chance of winning, right?

Now, how can you increase your chance of winning? Easy. You simply **flip the coin again**. Now you've DOUBLED your chances of coming up heads. The more you flip the coin, the more chances you have of winning.

Ok, I hear you. Seeing if a client has work is nowhere near a 50/50 proposition... most often, they don't have any availability... many times it can feel like getting a job is closer to 1 out of 50...or even 100! (Any role-players out there? Is there such as thing as a 100-sided die?) But even then, **no matter the odds... the more you "roll"... the BETTER your chances of getting in touch with a client at just the right time.**

Clients, their needs, and the fluctuations of schedules and timing might all seem like a randomized soup of chaos. And to those who don't know how this "Timing" works, it is... until we learn how to see it...**and even manipulate it.**

More Frequency Leads To More Clients

The more you can put yourself in front of a client, the **more likely** they are to see you - or even think of you - when they have availability. The key word here is "**frequency**". It's a simple equation: more frequency equals more clients, more work, and more success!

Here's the caveat: notice I said *"put yourself in front of a client."* That doesn't mean you should send a weekly email blast to every possible client you ever met saying *"Hey, ya got any work?"* That's a great way to get yourself ignored (and/or blocked).

What I mean is to **make yourself visible** on the channels where they hang out. Give them a hearty congrats on a work anniversary or promotion. Comment and like their posts. Post something about a job you recently completed. (Another shameless plug for LinkedIn here: it makes this super-easy!)

And... yes... on occasion, directly check in with them via email or messaging about how things are going, and to let them know you have some availability and would be happy to look at any project they might have coming up, to see if you can help. **Make it about you helping THEM, not them doing you a favor. There's a big difference.**

This is a huge mindset shift if you avoid talking to prospective clients, because maybe you feel "icky" or "salesy". If this is the case, try **changing your perspective to theirs.** How do *they* feel? If they genuinely are looking for good freelancers, then your courteous contact will be a welcome one.

Read the room here. If they respond with a terse, short answer, then maybe that's a sign that they don't like being directly contacted in that way. Move on. However, if they take the time to answer politely and thank you for reaching out, then that's a sign that they do appreciate the contact, and that they are someone you can check back in with in the future.

Any one of these little connections, which we can call "**touch points**", don't have to be a big deal... they can just be a small little micro-interaction. The quantity matters just as much as the quality.... Because these "touch points" stack up. **The more times your client sees your name, the more likely it is that they will remember you.**

This is a cornerstone of **branding**. The more often you manage to weasel your way into a client's mind, the more likely they will be to remember you. Most of the time they come across your name, they won't need your creative services. But when they *do* need you, they will start out by thinking to themselves, *"Now who do I know of that does that?"* When you've done your job right, your name may just be one of the first that pop into their head.

Tame Chance By Keeping Track Of Clients

Many freelancers come up short in the client department because **they don't have a process in place** to make sure that they reconnect with a client when the timing IS right. Several years ago I learned how truly important this is.

Back in 2023, due to a slowdown in business because of strikes in the production industry, I noticed that I wasn't getting as many emails asking for availability as I had before. I assumed this was due to the strikes making work more scarce… but that wasn't the full picture, as I would soon find out.

I decided to do a bit of research, and reviewed the clients I had worked with in the past few years. Sheepishly, I realized **I had never taken the time to properly keep track of them.** I hunted down the names and emails of all my clients, and any other info about them that I could find, and put them into my HubSpot CRM (Customer Management System).

During this process, I went back through several years of emails and made a shocking realization: **that there were**

several clients who had requested my time on multiple occasions, but no work ever came out of it. One potential client, who I had yet to work with, had requested for my availability no less than SIX times within a six month period! Eventually, they must have just given up because I hadn't heard from them after that.

This made me realize the need to reach out to "clients out in the cold" again and let them know that I was available and still really wanted to work with them. I also discovered that in some cases, there were key people that had **transitioned out of their previous place of work, and I needed to update my records to find out where they went.**

As I began to reach out to these "lost clients", I was happy to learn that they were grateful to hear back from me. While they were no longer with the same company, they were usually in a similar position at a different company and were glad to have an opportunity to update their list of freelancers. And it was a win-win exercise, as I ended up getting some work out of it… and *they* got to regain an awesome freelancer (me)!

"Bad timing" can cause you to give up and to discard the hard work you've invested in establishing a relationship to a potential client. ***Don't***! The story above helps both of us realize that a client is worth keeping track of… and reaching out to… even when it seems like every time you do, it isn't the right timing. Be patient and persistent: eventually it *will* be the right timing.

While we might blame our lack of clients on "bad timing", this externalizes the issue. Rather, when we ask ourselves, *"what can I do to tilt these odds in my favor?"* then we begin to take ownership of the problem – and we become empowered to find the solution. The foundation of that solution is keeping good records of where your clients are… and the persistence to keep it updated.

Take Advantage Of Your "Freshness" While You Have It

Have you ever noticed how awesome French fries are when they're fresh… and yet how incredibly *mediocre* they are just a handful of minutes later?

When they're right out of the fryer, there they are, all golden and crispy and irresistible. Many were the times when, on the way home from the burger joint after picking up a lazy dinner for the family, I found myself sneaking a few fries out of the bag. And then, by the time I got home with them just a few minutes later, they well on their way to becoming limp and soggy.

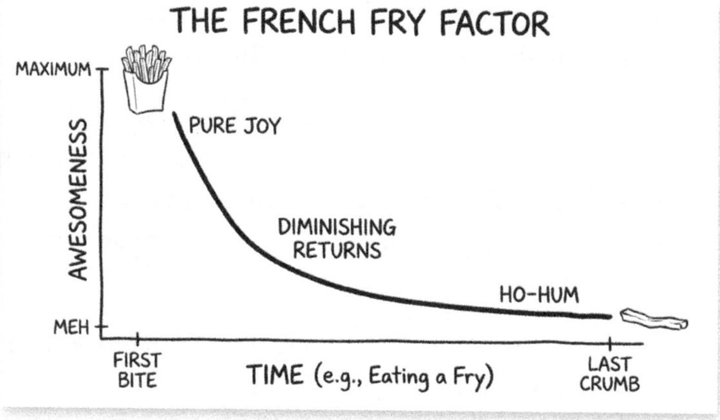

Many french-fried potatoes were sacrificed to bring you this statistical triumph of a chart.

Human nature seems to cause us to regard many things with the same kind of rapidly decaying attention. Our interest in a new thing, concept, or even person can peak at the beginning and then tail off rapidly over time.

When you make first contact with a potential client, it can often be this way… they seem interested in you at first, **and then it seems like things just "cool off"**… you don't hear from them again. Perhaps other things got in the way and they forgot about you. Don't be offended by this; it's how our brains work. Our attention is limited in scope, and it usually just has space enough for the most recent events.

Rather than be offended by it, *take advantage of it.* Part of the art of client timing is to acknowledge this human trait and harness the "freshness" while you have it. As the saying goes, **"strike while the iron is hot".**

This might mean that after an initial contact with a client, you **follow up** with them in a quick message or email. Tell them how much you enjoyed talking with them about their project, and that you look forward to the possibility of working with them. If there were any "open loops" created during your talk, such as a request for references or a link to your reel, **supply them with this information right away.**

To minimize the chance that you'll "go soggy" on them, **follow up a week later or so** with a brief message or email. If they ghost you, well, at least you did your part to remain relevant. They have your information; all you can do is move on to the next one.

Stay positive! In my experience, there have been times when a client seemed not very interested, and then one day out of the blue they contacted me about a project. Keep planting those seeds and eventually some of them will sprout. Just know that – unlike those limp fries – **there are things you can do to "stay fresh" in your clients' minds and extend your shelf life.**

Seven Tips To Help You Get In Sync With Your Clients

1. Have a client tracking system in place.

I've brought it up before, I know… But here it is again. Have a CRM or **some kind of process to keep track of your clients.** If you don't have this, then you're sifting through thousands of emails trying to find that person who worked at that place for that job you can't remember.

2. Set up a reminder to check back in with your clients.

If it's not the best time to work with a client, then ask when they think it would be a good time to check back in. Even if they really don't know when they will have jobs again (which they probably won't) then you've set up **an excuse to reconnect** at a later date. Set an automated reminder or date in your calendar, and check back at that time.

3. Repeatedly and consistently make yourself visible where your client hangs out.

Whenever your client sees you, it's yet another touch point in their mind that you exist. We've already touched on this in the Authority section, but assuming you already have taken those steps to have authority in the mind of your clients, this is about **frequency**. The more frequently they see you, the more likely they are to **think of you** when they do have work.

4. Learn the seasonal aspects of your client's industry or niche.

Many industries have times during the year when work is either slow to nil, or fast n' furious. **It pays to learn and monitor the seasonality** of your clients' business!

For example, years ago the studio I worked for at that time had a client who was a large toy company. Every spring we would help them get all their ads ready for a big industry convention called the Toy Fair. In the two months leading up to that event, there was a TON to do… and we hunted down **every single artist we could possibly find** to help with the workload.

More recently, a client I freelanced with had a lot of work around major sporting events, as their client was a major athletic shoe company. Things were quiet from them for a while but eventually the next year's sporting events began to roll around and… guess what? **Two weeks** before the event, they were **urgently looking** for freelancers again!

Now, you tell me – do you think a good time to check back in with a client like this is some random time during the summer when there are no sporting events… OR… would a good time be **a few weeks before** the next sporting event? (Seems like a good thing to put as an automatic reminder in my calendar…)

Speaking of summers, certain times of the year might be slower… usually summers and year-end holidays are a slower time as corporate clients take time off. These times can be great opportunities for freelancers who can step in whenever key personnel – like in-house creative staff – take their vacations, too. If you were to check in with a client "just in the nick of time" to capture these jobs, what time do you think would be best to reach out?

5. Have a policy in place to handle holidays and weekends.

If you need the work, then these highly valued time periods are great times to step in and fill a demand! Staff artists many times aren't willing to work these hours, and so companies have to tap into their freelancer list to fill this need. **Since these hours are considered more valuable, I definitely recommend charging overtime** for holidays and weekends. (I sure do!)

Having loved ones who understand and are flexible is key to this… obviously I would never recommend sacrificing personal relationships for work. BUT…

… on the *other* hand, many times a great paying gig is worth celebrating a holiday another day. So maybe you *don't* celebrate Valentine's Day on February 14th in a crowded restaurant like everyone else… BUT now you can afford that romantic out-of-town weekend! (Hey, if your spouse or significant other gets mad at this suggestion, it wasn't *my* idea…)

6. Don't give up… be consistent!

Keep at it! Don't give up on your clients, and don't expect them to give up on you. That magical-seeming thing called "synchronicity" between you and your clients might seem random, like luck. In truth, **it's simply a numbers game.** As you consistently check in with clients, and they check in with you, eventually your mutual interests WILL align and you'll get hired.

Learn everything you can about your clients' needs, their schedules, and their habits. Armed with this information, you can better put yourself in front of them at the right times, when they might be in need of a good freelancer.

*7. **Don't get discouraged!***

We humans have a lot going on… all the time. Be **polite**, be **patient**, and be **flexible** with your busy clients... and with yourself!

Remember, dealing with this kind of schedule and relationship stuff is something **people in business do all the time.** When you went freelance, you became a business, too… and you're the ***only*** one in your business who can do this stuff. Fortunately, if you follow the above tips, it will become much easier to get "in sync" with your clients needs.

And the more "in sync" you are with your clients… and the better you manage your timing… **the more magnetic you will become to them.**

Freedom From "Feast Or Famine" Freelancing

While many of us freelancers love what we do, one of the top downsides that we have is **inconsistency**. I've uncovered this in a lot of the research I've done, as well as drawing from my own experience. Much of the time, freelancing seems like it's "feast or famine"... jobs either pile on all at once, or we're sitting around waiting for the next job to happen. (And waiting....and waiting...)

As freelancers, we don't get that nice reliable check from an employer every two weeks like clockwork. For those of us who have experienced that, it's certainly a nice luxury! (Until that one day when it stops... that's pretty stressful when it happens, and I've been there, too.)

We can, however, achieve some degree of what I call "leveling out". These highs and lows of freelancing can be tamed to an extent if we put into practice what we've learned in this section on timing, especially when we pair it with **good habits.**

Good habits include things like staying up on your client outreach efforts consistently, even when you already are busy with a job at the time. **The best time to reach out to a client is actually *when* you're busy, not when you're looking for work.** Then you can say things like,

> ***"Hi, I'm currently on a project at the moment but I did want to reach out and let you know that I free up after March 14th, if you have any projects that you'd like to discuss."***

Perhaps you agree or not, but I think that sounds a **lot** better than this:

> ***"Hi there! I'm not working on anything at the moment... got any work?"***

The "rollercoaster" that is the job flow - and variable income - of freelancing *can* be tamed, after all, to some extent... with a good use of **timing** and **good habits** in maintaining contact with clients.

Synchronicity Leads To Success

Let's review what we talked about on Timing. It's extremely powerful when it comes to being in the right place at the right time for getting clients and building your freelance business.

While the art of client-getting might seem like chance, it can be manipulated in your favor by increasing the **frequency** with which your clients come into contact with you. These "touch points" all stack in your favor and work to put you top of mind when your client has a need that you can fill.

You can increase your odds of success by **tracking** - keeping consistent records - of these touch points and any other communication with your clients. This information provides valuable insight your clients and well as a source of data.

We also talked about some other tips on how you can get in sync with your clients, including things like setting up a **tracking system**, **reminders**, and well-thought out **policies** and **scripts** for how to handle special situations, like when clients ask about your availability on weekends or holidays.

(Speaking of scripts – it's bonus time again! I have a curated selection of pre-written scripts just for you in your bonuses section of the book website at: theclientmagnetmethod.com. *Feel free to use them after tweaking to suit your personality, taste, and voice.)*

Timing is a tool... learn how you can **use it to win**! If you do, you'll have a valuable asset with which you can grow your freelance business... as well as have a lot more consistency in your job flow. This will also help you minimize the "feast or famine" ups and downs that all freelancers face... while enjoying the other great benefits of having a great creative freelance business.

CHAPTER 6
CHARISMA

Is It Possible To Be More "Likable?"

Here's a simple fact I'd like to impress upon you. Do whatever you need to do to remember it every day. Write it down, put it next to your mirror so that you see it every morning, or write it on your forehead with a permanent marker (ok, maybe not that one.) Here it is:

If people LIKE you, you will get MORE freelance jobs.

There. I said it.

Yes, it feels kind of icky.

Yes, it reminds you of high school where you felt left out because you weren't in the "it" crowd.

No need to throw in the towel if you weren't one of those "popular people". I certainly wasn't one. Like many of you, I just used the time I spent not getting invited to parties sitting in my room being creative. It certainly paid off later in life!

While it didn't come naturally to me, I eventually tried to develop the skills to become a bit more "likable". People may call this different things... personality, or charisma, or communication skills. It may seem hard to pin down. **Let's just call it "charisma."**

With that out of the way, let's spend a bit of time clarifying what charisma is, shall we? Believe it or not, you might just find you have more than you thought...

What Charisma Is (And Isn't)

Now, before you scoff... I realize the word "charisma" has kind of a charged meaning. It might conjure up imagery of dime-store charlatans or sparkly, silver-tongued salesmen looking to sell you something you don't want.

Those examples (or any others that the word might conjure in your mind) are really more like an *abuse* of charisma... that doesn't mean that charisma itself is a bad thing. In the hands of a good people like you and me, it's a *great* thing! It can make our interactions with each other much smoother, and make us more attractive. It's not about being something we're not... rather, it's about **refining our image of who we really are.**

And sometimes it can even mean **taking down the barriers** that we might have designed to keep people out. I know, I'm getting into some psychology here... but many of us creative-types (and I know us well) deliberately have ways to isolating ourselves from others so we can go into our happy creative place, where we feel safe creating alone. We might have developed habits, appearances, and mannerisms that (intentionally or not) **deflect people**… the exact *opposite* of attracting them.

If I were to define charisma for our purposes, I'd say that while *communication* is the nuts and bolts of how we relate to each other, *charisma* is the **level of quality, believability, and attractiveness that you convey with HOW you communicate.** Communication gets the job done… but charisma **leads, persuades**, and even **inspires**.

If you don't feel like this is something you have or are good at, then read on… because what I have to say about this might just change your mind. Charisma is just another skill, and it **can be learned**. *Anybody* can improve their charisma.

Hey, I don't expect you to run for a political office or anything… but if you put a little effort into improving your charisma, then your prospective clients will see that you're someone they could enjoy working with.

Perhaps more importantly, **the hard work you've spent over the years to become an accomplished artist won't be overshadowed by a seemingly superficial set of negative impressions you might give to a prospective client.**

Let me share a real story that illustrates that I'm trying to say.

The Story Of "Awkward Andy"

A number of years ago, the company I was with wanted to hire some artists for an upcoming project, our biggest yet. The person tasked with finding them (we'll call her Emma) was a bit inexperienced in our industry, and she asked me to help since I knew what kind of talent and qualifications we were looking for. I had a conversation with one artist (we'll call him Andy) who was, in my opinion, clearly a great fit. I passed him along to Emma.

She came back in after their phone interview and told me the results. Apparently, **Andy had bombed it!** She said that she just "didn't like him." Confused, I talked with Emma to find out more. Eventually I was able to discover that she just felt he was "awkward to talk to". He seemed a bit gruff and even impolite to her. Sure, in our visit Andy seemed a bit, shall we say, "lacking in conversational polish". As a fellow creative nerdy-type, I was able to look past that and see Andy's talents as an asset to our company… but Emma wasn't.

I politely stood my ground, and strongly recommended that we hire Andy. It was a good thing, **because he went on to become one of our best artists.** He got us through a really crazy time of growth… not just with his excellent artistic and technical skills, but also his willingness and ability to learn new ones.

As for his personality, people actually really enjoyed being around his quirky humor… and he even met the love of his life while working for us and got married! (While I've never considered myself a matchmaker, I certainly am proud of that… because I had recommended hiring his significant other, too!)

The moral of the story here isn't "don't judge a book by its cover." Because you already know that. Unfortunately, most clients do NOT adhere to this mantra. Their business is all about judging covers. You can't change them… **but you *can* change YOU.**

The moral for you is, "don't let other people judge YOU negatively by stuff you can improve."

If "Awkward Andy" hadn't had me there, he wouldn't have gotten the job, and he wouldn't have found the love of his life! I'm not saying I'm a superhero or anything, but he dodged a bullet. On the other hand, if he had worked on his conversational and people skills, and made a bit of an effort to be more charismatic, enabling him to be more friendly to Emma, then he wouldn't have needed me to step in and bail him out.

Dealing With The "Emmas"

Companies - and organizations in general - are FULL of Emmas. Bless their hearts, they're pretty much good folks. But many of them are entry-level people who are inexperienced at hiring. They generally possess good people skills, that's why they got the job… **but that doesn't mean they know how to look past the superficial stuff and determine the best people for the jobs they're hiring for.**

One of your most important skills as a freelancer is **how effectively you communicate** to the Emmas of this world. They're often your first point of contact with a company. They have roles like "HR Coordinator", "Resourcing Manager", "Talent Acquisition Manager", or similar job titles. They might belong to a younger generation than you do, so they don't always have the same cultural points of contact as you.

These people are essentially **facilitators**, and are there to find people like you. Their purpose is to match a skilled professional with the needs of the job description handed to them by their supervisors. Once they've done that, they're tasked with facilitating the connection by onboarding you into their system, or they might hand that duty off to an HR-type person if they're with a larger company. Or, if there's more of a process there, they might hand you off to someone who you might be working with directly, such as a supervisor, project manager, or producer.

Emmas are also gatekeepers. They receive a lot of communication from multiple sides, and they're expected to sift through the tens or hundreds of people in order to find the right person. If it sounds like a stressful job, it usually is! As you can imagine, **if you can figure out the ways you can be more magnetic to them, then you can shoot right to the front of the line.** Being magnetic to them doesn't really have much to do with the job description either, but it might have to do with "charisma factors": your personality, your level of friendliness, and your timeliness in responding to them.

Now this is *really* not anything we learned in art or design school, is it? Well, like they say: better late than never! I learned this the hard way. You can learn the hard way, too, if you wish… or you can read the next bit and save yourself a lot of time and trouble.

Learning The "Soft Skills" Can Earn "Hard Cash"

Communication and stuff like this typically go into a category of skills that people tend to call "**soft skills**". They're called that because they can be "squishy"– difficult to define. But nobody can deny that **people who can communicate clearly and effectively, and who are likable, tend to be more successful.**

If you find yourself in online meetings with a client and it seemed to go well but in the end they didn't end up hiring you, maybe it was the way you came across personally. Or, maybe as you work with people, you feel like you have trouble saying what you want to say, or you feel weird about the interaction afterwards.

If this sounds like you, then you might consider looking into improving your charisma. If you invest in yourself in this way, you'll find your **confidence will grow dramatically.** As a result, your client interactions will go much more smoothly… and you'll **win more freelance gigs** because of it. Not only that, but you may find the **quality of your freelancing (and your life) improves substantially.**

Your Personality Can Be Your Competitive Advantage

By and large, **your work** can be replicated. **You** can't.

Debatably, much of the work you do can pretty much be done by any number of freelancers – or, now, even robots. So how do you avoid becoming a commodity? One way is **by having the kind of personality that people enjoy being around.**

Many freelancers (and creatives as a whole) don't care about this, believing that doing their job is all that matters, and so they **don't make any effort** to make themselves more likable. Some creatives even think being off-putting, moody, or negative is a *plus*, and that it *helps* their credibility.

You, on the other hand, have an advantage! You have this book in your possession, and you now have knowledge that it IS important to be "likable" … that it affects your ability to get work, your income, and even your career and personal satisfaction. You will probably find that with just a little bit of effort, you can make pretty huge improvements in your level of charisma and shoot ahead of the pack.

Ok, ok… now that I've used *my* incredible charisma to convince you, how do we go about improving *yours*?

How To Improve Your Charisma

1. Be Polite.

These days it seems like **politeness** is considered **optional**.

Maybe I'm old-fashioned. I grew up as a southern boy, being taught to say "please" and "thank you". I think it's interesting, though, that while many people claim that stuff's not very important, **it does seem to carry weight in their evaluations of people**. They might not give anybody "politeness points", but they will certainly be quick to judge when someone comes off as **rude**.

So… **be polite**. Greet people. Say please and thank you. Say goodbye, and tell them you look forward to your next conversation with them. There's a reason that centuries of human conversation have distilled these simple verbal practices into our interactions with each other – because they make us feel like the other person cares enough about us to say them.

And maybe that's what's really at work here… politeness (or the lack of it) really **makes the other person aware of how you feel about them.** In our very short texts and conversations with each other, our actual word count is pretty low. When you use some of that precious word-space to make the other person aware that you consider them a good fellow human being, then I think it's worth it.

2. Communicate Clearly.

A wise man once said, *"the quality of your life is the quality of your communication."* **We humans are essentially social creatures.** Even for those of use who like to hole up and create stuff for hours on end, it's important to "come up for air" every now and then… to **touch base with our clients and let them know how things are going.** Don't just wait for them to always initiate contact… **take the initiative** every once in a while.

Also, I hope that I don't offend anyone reading this, but if I did not address this then I would be doing you a disservice. Here it is: **strive to communicate effectively in the language your clients are primarily speaking**. I've encountered freelancers over the years who are insanely talented and capable, and yet they get overlooked in various ways because they aren't quite fluent enough in the language of the clients who are hiring them. I always hate seeing this, because it's of course terribly unfair… but in the world of clients, their goal isn't to be fair, their goal is to get their job accomplished.

If you do struggle with language barriers, there are a lot of ways you can improve… you can join a conversation group, take specialized training, or take one of the many language courses out there. With technology on our side, there are no longer any real obstacles to doing this other than our time and our willingness to improve.

3. Be Concise.

While communicating clearly is very important to your charisma, it's also vital to be *concise* - which is **communicating efficiently**. This means speaking and writing in ways that **aren't overly wordy, defensive, or over-explanatory.**

A few years ago, the studio I was with hired a freelance producer to help us get through a very busy period. I found pretty quickly that **this person was extremely stressful to interact with.** Whenever they sent an email, I would find myself tensing up because I was in for a long, confusing read, and if I didn't reply quickly enough they would hunt me down and talk to me at length, taking me out of my valuable productive work time.

They were very intelligent and had a lot of industry experience, but their style of communication was extremely **long and tedious**… when something would take one sentence to say, they would use ten or twenty sentences. They could become **defensive** very easily and ramble, **over-explaining** themselves. Apparently I wasn't the only one that found this troublesome… their emails to clients were tomes of near-unreadability. This producer ended up being let go from the gig early and was never asked back!

Your clients are busy people and they have things to do. **They will appreciate being communicated with in a way that respects that.** Less is more. Don't be defensive and don't over-explain. Be accurate and concise, while saying the things you need to say (and leave room for politeness, of course!)

4. Be Empathetic.

Deep down, **we all seek to be understood**, to be seen in a way that puts us in a light that feels **real and authentic to who we are.** This is such a fundamental need that when we are *not* understood (or, worse, *mis*understood) this can be very **stressful**, particularly in relationships!

Your clients are no different. If you want to be incredibly charismatic to them, then **make them feel like you understand them.** Rather than faking it by *pretending* to understand, it's best to understand in a *genuine* way… and this requires **empathy**.

Empathy is **stepping into another person's shoes and seeing things from their perspective.** How do they feel? What are their hopes, dreams, desires? What are their challenges, their frustrations? If this sounds too "unprofessional", too "touchy-feely", then perhaps this distance is the reason you haven't been getting the ideal clients you want!

(If you did the **client avatar exercise** and walked through the *Client Field Guide* with me from the third chapter on Positioning, then you've built a solid foundation for deeply understanding – and empathizing with – your clients. If you haven't done this yet, consider **downloading the Client Field Guide** at **theclientmagnetmethod.com** and working through these exercises. I guarantee it's worthwhile!)

The Key: Focus On Your Clients (Not Yourself)

Being creative, out of necessity, **involves a lot of "self".** Our creative output is very personal to us. This is why it's so tough to put ourselves out there and show our work to people, and to receive critical feedback about it. But in the marketing stage of freelancing, when we've created the thing and we're ready to show it, **we have to put the "self" part in the backseat for awhile and focus on the person viewing, considering, and consuming our creative output.**

I know this can be tough, especially when we feel sensitive about our work. Many of us are pretty introverted to begin with, which certainly doesn't make it easy! All I can say is, **it does get better with time and experience.** The more you interact with clients and show your work to them and talk about it, the more comfortable you are likely to be with it. And as you build your own confidence, it's easier to focus on the other person and be empathetic.

With each and every interaction, be sure that **every sentence puts your client as the star of the show,** as the center of their own mini-universe. Yes, we all know you're talented… they suspect you are, too, or they wouldn't be talking to you… so you don't have to keep proving yourself or telling them how talented you are. Show them that you're genuinely interested in them.

Talk less and listen more. Determine to clarify the other person's needs. Make absolutely sure you understand them, and that you know what their goals for the project are. They might actually not know precisely what their goals are… and when you help them clarify them, it makes them realize that you can help them.

"Understanding" is a key word here. Remember, we all innately seek to be understood. Real listening is almost a lost art form these days. So **when you listen intently to your clients' needs, and genuinely seek to understand them, this is incredibly magnetic!**

5. Manage Your Nerves.

When we feel nervous, we tend to exhibit neurotic behaviors like over-explaining, speaking too fast, questioning ourselves, and over-apologizing. We trail off the end of our sentences, or put inflections on them so that every statement sounds like a question. In our over-eagerness to be understood, we might even interrupt our client when they're speaking.

When you act nervous, **it makes other people nervous, too,** and makes for an unpleasant conversation. Work on some relaxation techniques before a conversation. Be sure to breathe, and pace your speech, not trying to talk too fast. Realize that you are qualified to help the person you're talking to, and that you're equals seeking a mutual business relationship.

Acting nervous might sound like it only applies to video-conferencing or in-person contact, but it can affect our written communication, too. It can cause us to over-share or be too wordy, or come across as defensive (for example, the story of the producer I shared earlier!)

6. Be Confident.

Confidence is perhaps the most difficult… and the most misunderstood… of all these charisma factors.

Confidence doesn't come across when you're nervous, as we just described… when you're nervous, you're doing the *opposite* of inspiring confidence in your clients. So getting rid of the nerves, as well as the nervous habits that go along with them, goes a long way here.

Another important point: **confidence is not is "cockiness"**. This is going overboard, being OVER-confident by making exaggerated claims without offering to back them up. People can tell when someone is all bluster and bluff. Just because people don't get called out for being artificially confident, that doesn't mean their artificiality doesn't get noticed. While it might appear to work in the short term, it's not a viable long-term method of instilling confidence in your abilities.

True confidence, rather, is **the strong sense that you are highly capable of performing the job that your prospective client needs done.** This doesn't come from telling them, but by ***showing*** them.

"Show, don't tell" is a storyteller's mantra that's a surefire method of making people personally invested in whatever message you're trying to communicate. It works because it causes them to expend a little bit of their own energy to answer the questions they have about how you can help them … so it's *active* rather than passive.

For example, when you have the things in place that we talked about in the previous chapter on Authority, such as a well-crafted body of work, then that invites your clients to assess those materials and **decide for themselves** whether or not you're capable of doing the creative job they need done.

Another important element of confidence is **the way you present yourself.** It's having the qualities of **calmness,**

strength, and **self-control.** It says, *"hey, I've been here before, I've got this."* It instills a high degree of certainty in your clients without resorting to false claims or bravado. If you don't have confidence in what you do, or if you think you have it but don't have the skills to back it up, then a moment will eventually arise to test you!

I had to learn confidence very early in my career. I would sit in a room with clients, working with material that was being displayed on a large screen right in front of them. As you can imagine, this could be a high-stress situation, especially when a deadline loomed and I had multiple people in the room with conflicting personalities! Getting good at what I did was of course essential... but even more than that, **I also had to learn how to *appear* (and feel) confident,** in order to **inspire** confidence in my clients.

My mentor in those days described it as being like a **commercial airline pilot.** This was an analogy that really helped me at the time. The "passengers" (clients) can't fly the plane themselves... they are relying on YOU to do that. Can you imagine the passengers' reaction if the pilot came on the intercom and sounded nervous? They would start freaking out! In extreme cases, the passengers might even feel so scared that the pilot can't perform their job of flying the plane that they try to break into the cockpit and wrestle the controls away!

Your job as an artist is to use your skills to 'land the plane' safely. And just like a pilot, it's important to **convey your confidence** in doing so. (Maybe those airline pilots are overcompensating, and that's why they always sound half asleep whenever they talk through the intercom!)

"But... What If I Don't FEEL Confident?"

Many times in our creative journey we don't feel like we are able to do something. In fact, that's pretty much the par for the course for a creative person… we see something we're not sure we can do, we do it anyway, and then we succeed. Sure, that's a gross over-simplification, there are many more bumps in the road than that, but that's essentially the process.

So **how are we supposed to BE confident if we don't FEEL confident?** This conjures up the old, often-used phrase *"fake it 'till you make it"*.

Sure, I don't really care for that phrase, either. But it's essentially what we have to do to some degree if we want to ever level up our creative career. If we didn't, then we would always stay stuck at the same place. Change and progress doesn't happen in the comfort zone, where it's "safe" and predictable. **The magic happens *outside* the comfort zone.**

I'm not saying to take on something that you're totally unqualified to tackle. What I'm saying is, learn how your skills and successful past experiences apply to new situations and opportunities. Review your past successes, and note how you overcame obstacles in order to achieve things. Give yourself some credit! Hopefully this doesn't sound trite but I'll say it anyway: ***you got this.***

Find an **example** to follow. In the earlier example of my mentor, it helped when I visualized a pilot. When I was a little kid, I wanted to be a pilot, so I already admired them… it was relatively easy to act like one. There was also a creative director I had back in those days who clients absolutely seemed to love. I was always fascinated watching him in meetings with clients, how he inspired their confidence.

Needless to say, he had a high degree of charisma and he was a great example for me. Find someone you admire who can be a good example for you, too.

Confidence also *naturally* occurs through **experience**. Feeling confident will get easier as you progress in your professional career and level up. Remember the **Four Stages of Competence from Chapter 1** in this book? When you attain mastery in the various areas of your creative career, and reach that blissful level of Unconscious Competence, you can't *help* but be confident.

Always strive to be improving, learning, and succeeding. You've got the skills to pay the bills. You have capabilities that people are willing to pay you to use to help them. Own it!

7. Be Positive.

Some people, many of them creative-types, have adapted the style of a **pessimist** that sees the world as a glass half-empty. They are habitual naysayers, people who are quick to point out why something won't work, or offer a negative comment. They often exude a "negative energy" that resonates in their speech and body language.

(For some reason, many of these people tend to congregate on Reddit, and for that reason I'd advise limiting your exposure to that particular platform! Any Redditor freelancers here? Let's hear from ya! I'd love it if you created a post to this book and flambéed me. I'd be honored, actually.)

Hopefully this statement about the negative aspects of being negative won't offend you if you pride yourself as someone with this style, but I'm just going to be honest with you when

I say that **negativity isn't going to get as many clients or win as many jobs.**

You don't have to be bubbly, over-excited, or Pollyanna-esque. I'm not asking you to be fake – people will usually see right through that. What I am saying is that to win the job, you may need to demonstrate in your conversations with potential clients that you are positive that you can *do* the job, and do it well. **Express your positivity and confidence, and your client will feel positive and confident in you.**

When, during the course of working with the client, things go south and you encounter obstacles (as you inevitably will) then **don't make a big deal about them.** Show you're a problem solver and get it done. When you're positive, then the overall impression people have of you will be positive, and you'll get clients calling you back again and again.

8. Be Reliable.

This is another foible that I see a lot in my fellow creatives: **they're just not very reliable**. This is not something unique to younger, more inexperienced ones, either… I've also seen it in creatives who have been pros for years. **Being someone who is reliable - in addition to your creative talents, of course - will make you extremely attractive to your clients.**

Some creatives believe that their talent and experience give them license to slack off in other areas, such as not being on time to meetings, failing to meet deadlines, or lack of follow-through on their claims that they can do something. Well, your clients might not tell you so to your face, but **they don't like it when they feel that they can't rely on you.** You're a freelancer, a temp for hire - why would they do the uncomfortable task of confronting you about it when all they have to do is just make it through this project with you and then just decide to never call you again?

Being reliable basically means that **you're going to do what you said you will do**. For example, when you accept a meeting request, you're essentially saying that you'll be at the meeting when it starts. If you don't show up, then you've taken a hit to your credibility as well as your integrity. **Every action - or lack of action - sends a message.** When you allow yourself to be someone who can't be relied upon, what message do you think you're sending to your clients?

This might sound a bit harsh… and I'm being this way because **I was once … (gasp!) … unreliable**. I did *all* of those things when I was much younger… and even years into my career. I guess I thought my talent made up for it. One day, I woke up and smelled the coffee – and realized that what I thought was cute wasn't so cute to anybody else. Part of this realization was that I was being passed over for conversations, meetings, and even jobs. In one case, my lack of attention - and failure to care enough to remember a meeting - even damaged a friendship that never recovered from it.

I hope you don't think any less of me as a person for having a history of struggling with this. (Hey, I'm human, too!) The good news is, after learning some very important (and difficult) lessons I've turned it around… it's make a huge positive difference. I can say with certainty that my clients now see me as rock-solid, someone they can depend on, and, yes, it has resulted in a lot of success.

Reliability Increases Trust; Unreliability *Decreases* Trust.

It's a pretty simple formula, really. Reliability is intimately connected with something we discussed earlier in Chapter 2 on Authority, and that's **trust. We become magnetic and attractive when we attain a state of trust with our clients.** Failing to be someone that they can rely on does the opposite, it moves us *out* of that state of trust… and instead of being magnetic, **you become *repulsive*.** Eew! As in, perma-banned, ghosted, dropped like a hot potato. (Sure, repulsive is a strong word, but after all, it *is* the opposite of magnetic!)

You might find that a few little simple adjustments to your habits here can pay off in spades. **Here are some suggestions that can rocket your reliability factor to eleven… and help you to become one of those select few freelancers that get on your clients' "first call" list.**

Meetings

Set reminders on your phone that go off when it's time to prepare for and attend a meeting. **Show up a few minutes early.** If it's a remote meeting via Zoom or some sort of tele-conferencing (and these days they usually are!) Then give yourself time to ensure that your mic and video are working properly in those couple of minutes before the call.

Being a little early has a lot of great side-benefits, anyway… like chatting about what the weather's like where you are, what kind of coffee you're sipping on, or the name of the pet who's snoozing in their pet bed behind you! These little moments are rare, especially in a remote-work world, and they go a long way to fostering great relationships with your fellow coworkers, no matter how short your time with them might be.

Time Estimates

Pretty much every job has that special client who's always asking the question: "How long will it take you?" They're also the ones who, while you're in the middle of concentrating on getting a task delivered, will ping you several times asking, *"Not to bother you, but .... how's it going? What time do you think you'll be done?"*

One thing that I've always struggled with as a creative is estimating how long it will take me to do something, and managing my time effectively along the way. A lot of us do! Creative work is often very difficult to quantify. In my eagerness to tell people what they want to hear, I would often quote that it would take me less time than it should have. It took me awhile to learn that while they might like hearing it, it puts you (*and* them) in a stressful and hard to manage situation right off the bat.

Experience here is the best teacher. After a while you'll learn how fast it will take you to do things. When under the gun and a deadline is looming, use this as an opportunity to give the creative side of your brain a little break – lean back in your chair, close your eyes a moment, take a deep breath, and objectively **assess your situation.**

Consciously shift your thoughts from the right side of your brain (creative) to the **left side (analytical)**. Think about the task you have ahead of you and assess the time it will take. Pad that estimate with some extra so that you have a bit of wiggle room… not too much, of course, but just a bit more than what you *think* it will take. Let them know, and then continue on your work.

If you tend to struggle with **perfectionism**, it will be extra difficult to finish your tasks and meet deadlines. This will require some honest insight and self-work, because perfectionism (and yes, I'm a recovering perfectionist, too!) is almost always about one thing: **fear**.

We may hide behind perfectionism, and even wear it as a badge of honor, when really we're just **afraid of delivering our work**. Delivering opens us up to criticism and rejection. Learn how to be okay with that, how to manage that fear, and you'll be on your way to recovering from perfectionism… as well as being that reliable freelancer who delivers.

Work Estimates

While you might be a pro in your creative field, there might be some specializations within your particular niche that you feel less proficient in. **Be as honest with yourself as possible - and with your clients, when appropriate - about these limitations.**

For example, in my creative niche, I can do a number of tasks, including video editing, compositing, visual effects, color correction, graphic design, and motion design. Someone who hires me might assume that I can do all of these things, and many freelancers in my field can… **but everybody's better at some disciplines than others.**

Personally, out of all the things I do, I'd say that I'm not as strong in color correction. I'm not as fast at it, it's not super-intuitive, and I have to lean on tools like color scopes and measurements to help me. I'm upfront about this when it's relevant or if the topic comes up, and it's never really a problem, especially since color is nearly always handled by another kind of artist anyway… but the fact that I was **honest about my capabilities** goes a long way towards instilling confidence in my clients. They then get to decide if my color capabilities are strong enough for the job at hand, or if they need to hand it off to someone else.

Be as **accurate as possible**, while also being willing to better yourself and learn any areas that you might feel you need to improve. If you do, you'll find that your clients will appreciate your candor, and they'll come to trust your judgement on these things. They'll consider you **more and more reliable** as you successfully complete jobs with them.

9. Be Responsive.

Being responsive is simply **how quickly you respond** to things like messages and emails from your clients, and it certainly impacts how reliable they perceive you to be.

When I started freelancing, I found out in a hurry that I had better get people's names and contact information down right away in my contacts list - or else I'd miss their messages. A few little tweaks to my habits (there's that "habit" word again!) and how I use the "virtual assistant" that is my smartphone did the trick here… and now I rarely miss a message.

Clients often use different technologies to message one another… in my field they mostly use either Microsoft Teams or Slack. I make sure that **notifications are turned on** for these apps, as well as for my email. I also make sure they're **set as "VIP" contacts** in my email program so that they will always get through any possible spam filters. When the day's work starts and it's time to be "available", I make sure that my overall **notifications are set to "Work" status** so that I see and hear them.

I make it a game to try and respond as soon as possible, often within seconds. It's often funny to see a client's surprise when I do respond so quickly, and also it tells me that other freelancers must have set the bar pretty low for them. (I should offer a caveat here... I only do this during "working hours" unless during special cases when I might be expected to work late. It's important to **be clear with your clients about expectations of when you'll be available**... as well as boundaries!)

10. Follow The Golden Rule.

If you happen to be in the moment and you forget any of these charisma items, then just be sure to at least remember this one: the **Golden Rule**.

(No, the Golden Rule isn't "who has all the gold makes the rules"... although I admit, you could make a case for that!)

This fits right in with what we discussed earlier about **empathy**: putting yourself in someone else's shoes. It's a freelancer's greatest superpower!

Simply ask yourself, *"if I were this person, or if I were in their position, how would I want to be treated?"* Or, to to look at it another way: *"if I were this person and looking for the ideal freelancer to do the work they need done, what qualities would inspire confidence... and make me want to work with them?"*

If you remember that one simple rule, which pretty much encapsulates all those other rules, then you'll be on the right track!

Remember... *Anybody* Can Improve Their Charisma.

Anyone can become more likable with a bit of practice. And if you feel uncomfortable, that's totally expected! Changing any ingrained habits like this can feel awkward. That's why I recommend a bit of purposeful learning and practice.

Time for a personal share here. Back when I was a teenager, I used to be SUPER awkward, and I had terrible charisma. It was awful. I avoided interactions with people. It was just NOT a good time. (Having a low self-confidence didn't help much either!)

I purposely **made an effort** to improve my charisma, and found out how. Later in my career I **joined a group called Toastmasters**, which improved my ability to talk to other people and feel more confident doing so. They're probably known for helping people with public speaking, but they actually helped me develop a number of people and even leadership skills. I found it to be an incredibly nurturing and supportive environment where I could learn and practice these new skills.

It helped tremendously, and continues to benefit me any time I interact with people, including clients. I actually look forward to meetings with them… and I truly enjoy working with them.

So **let's review** what we learned about Charisma, and how it helps your freelancing business.

First, we talked about what Charisma is, how it's often misunderstood, and why it's important to strive to **be more "likable" if you want to be magnetic** to your ideal clients.

Making an effort to develop your **Charisma**, and what are known as "**soft skills"**, can become your "secret weapon" in your business, as you become someone your clients will want to work with again and again… not just because you get the job done, but because they find it pleasant to interact with you.

Next we discussed some concrete ways that we can work on improving our charisma, such as **politeness**, **communicating clearly**, **empathizing** with them, being **concise**, and the importance of **focusing on our clients' needs.** We also talked about **managing our nerves** and how to **attain more confidence** in our interactions with clients, **being positive**, and how to be seen as **reliable**. We also discussed the "**golden rule**" and how keeping it top of mind makes all these other things easier.

Improve your charisma, and it can dramatically improve your freelancing business. As a result, you will become more magnetic to your clients. The natural result is *more* clients, more bookings, and more income. And, don't forget a great bonus that improved charisma gives you… **it improves the quality of your life every day in your interactions with other people.**

CHAPTER 7
NETWORK

Your Network Works To Get YOU Work

Here we are, the last of the "magnificent seven" Client Magnet Methods… your **Network**!

This one may be last in the list, but it is definitely not least. Being the last item we talk about in this book is fitting, though… because it can take longer to develop after you've grown your freelancing for a while. After a period of time, when your network has reached a certain level of maturity, it reaches a "critical mass" and begins maintaining itself with a minimum of effort.

Your network is a **valuable business asset** that's **constantly working in the background** for you to get you clients and win you more creative freelance jobs. It also acts as a **resource** that you can tap into, like a never-ending rich vein of gold, whenever you need work, advice, referrals, or any number of "boosters" to grow your business.

How a Robust Network Benefits Creative Freelancers

- *Referrals and Recommendations:*

A strong network increases the likelihood of receiving referrals and recommendations from satisfied clients or collaborators.

- *Collaborative Opportunities:*

Opportunities for collaborations with other freelancers or professionals in your network can lead to more diverse and higher-profile projects.

- *Industry Insights:*

A robust network provides access to valuable industry insights, keeping you informed about trends, best practices, and potential opportunities.

- *Client Trust and Confidence:*

Clients are more likely to trust and hire freelancers with a strong network, as it reflects positively on their reputation and reliability.

- *Continuous Learning:*

Networking allows freelancers to learn from others in the industry, stay updated on new technologies, and enhance their skills.

- *Community Support:*

Being part of a network provides emotional support, advice, and encouragement, especially during challenging times in a freelancer's career.

So how do you develop and grow this Network, this magnificent organism that does all these wondrous things?

Well, we turn the noun "network" into a verb: "**networking**". (Ugh, things just got more business-y, didn't they?)

Not to fear. Networking can be fun, and it doesn't have to feel "business-y" at all. Read on for some practical tips and habits you can incorporate into your daily freelancing journey that makes growing your network easy.

Think of the process of growing your network as **planting seeds**. It's a long game. When you do a little bit each day, and do these things for every client and every job you encounter, you'll grow your network into a formidable force before you know it. In fact, many of the things we already talked about in this book, when you do them, will do a lot of the heavy lifting for you… you just need to incorporate a few things into it to make it more purposely work for you.

Know (And Reconnect With) Your *Existing* Leads and Clients

When I first rebooted my freelancing career, I thought my method of keeping track of my past clients and client leads was good enough. This method consisted of putting a star next to their name in my email app, and saving them in my contacts list. I also maintained a text document with the names of all the people that I'd worked with. I was connected with some of them on LinkedIn, but not all.

This is what I'd consider "intermediate level" client tracking… it did the trick to an extent. But it was not a living, breathing **process**... it required me to remember to do it, and once I put them down, what if their information changed? I began to realize my client tracking process was not quite up to snuff - I had let a lot of clients fall through the cracks.

Earlier I had mentioned that when things slowed down due to some industry strikes recently, I began to go through my old emails. What I found surprised me... there were clients that had reached out to me... and I had forgotten to star their name or put them in my contact list! Also... to my horror... i saw that **some of them had emailed me, and I never emailed them back!**

This alone was enough to make me step up my game... and I did. I searched for a good CRM (Customer Relationship Management) tool that worked well for single freelancers like me. I decided to go with **HubSpot**. A nice bonus: it's free!

I spent the better part of the next couple of weeks going through my old emails and notes and entering every single client I had worked with into my new system. I made more illuminating discoveries - such as finding out that some of my best clients were no longer at their jobs! Some had moved over to other companies, but I just had their old email. I reached out to them to touch base and see how they were doing, and to politely ask for their new email address.

This is where **LinkedIn** was a real lifesaver... it gave me a method to contact these clients without even having their current email. It also gave me a great excuse to reach out to them. And... pretty much all of them responded with their email and were glad that I reached out. (Sorry, I couldn't help but throw in another shameless LinkedIn plug there!)

Your leads are very valuable because they already know you, even if you haven't gotten to work with them yet. Your **past paying clients**, though, are **MANY times more valuable**, because they already know you and have work history with you. **Don't let them fall through the cracks!**

Know Who's Who In Your Niche - And Connect With Them

After you've catalogued every client, go on a mission to **get the names and current contact information of any and every possible client in your niche.** This may sound obvious, but you'd be surprised at how many freelancers don't think this is important… and as a result they don't even know who their potential (or even existing) client base is.

A great place to start is the immediate vicinity of your **current** clients and prospects. Look at **who else** you can connect with who works at same company. You can also look at companies *they've* worked at before, since those usually are in the same industry. It's actually kind of fun to go down these rabbit holes and find all these connections, and who has worked with who. (Guess what? They're doing the same thing from their side… and seeing your name as a connection to people THEY know. Now are you beginning to understand how powerful this is?)

As you widen your circle of contacts, you're widening the net of possible clients. **And as you strengthen those connections, you're making your network stronger.**

When you connect with people, this is where social media shines… this is what it's made for. Just be focused about it, and don't get sucked into the "time warp" of cat gifs and foodie pics. That's why LinkedIn is so great because it keeps the focus on the professional. (There I went again about LinkedIn, I just can't help myself.)

Keeping Your Connections "Warm"

I know I kind of bagged on some social media platforms where you might spend a lot of time following and interacting with your peers. I just didn't want you to use this as your ONLY method of looking for clients, or expecting immediate work to flood in. **Social media can certainly be a great channel for keeping in touch** with fellow freelancers as well as past clients, and so reaching out to them in some form, a little bit each day, *can* be super helpful.

Think of your "spiderweb" of various professional connections as existing **on a spectrum** between "warm" or "cold". The warmest connections are the ones whom you've already worked with on successful freelance gigs, and the people who you have interacted with most recently. These connections go "colder" the more time passes after interacting with them. You can **instantly warm up** a cold connection simply by checking in with them to see how they're doing, or by leaving an encouraging comment on a post they've made.

Since one of the great things about social media platforms is their visibility, you can even "warm" up **a lot of people at once by creating a social media post yourself,** or to a lesser extent commenting on a post. Multiple people in your network will see this and think, *"oh, yeah, that Mike guy is still around… cool!"* (Or, at least, you HOPE they will think things like that!)

In addition to social media, I have an **"inner circle" of other freelancers** who I consider not just peers, but friends. These are special folks what I might not even connect with on a job or anything, but I might text them or email them about something totally unrelated to work. That's what friends do, after all! This "inner circle" is usually where I go to first when a client needs a freelancer need that I can't fill.

Having a **warmed up network** will yield dividends in ways that will pay off when you least expect it. I have certainly referred other freelancers to clients, and I have also gotten work from my peers and friends who have done the same. There's nothing more fun than getting that text out of the blue with a new, exciting job right when you needed it. Some people call that luck… I call that a well-warmed network!

Being A Friendly Neighborhood Freelancer

As you grow through your freelance career, you start as a caterpillar in its larval stage, crawling around, not knowing anybody. As you complete successful jobs and build your network of connections, you soon become a butterfly that can fly around all over the place, connecting with all kinds of people.

Aspire to be the butterfly. Be a connector of people. Be a catalyst. Be a person of value. It's fun, and it cements you as a go-to person in your industry.

When you come across someone looking for a gig, offer a word of encouragement… or, better yet, a referral. When you come across a client who has moved jobs, had a birthday, or gotten let go, interact with them accordingly with a nice word or two. When you come across a client looking for a creative freelancer and you're already booked, give them someone's name you know can help them. When you see that someone has posted their work or is celebrating, pitch in and respond.

A little bit of this each day will go a long way towards **building your network**… strand by strand… person by person.

Attend Networking Events

Some events are related to your niche, and some aren't. If you live in a metropolitan area, there might be quite a few of these. Attend the ones you feel would be helpful… but even if you find yourself at a networking event you don't think will yield you clients, **keep your mind open.** You never know what seeds you plant will yield fruit down the line.

Here's an important tip about networking events: **have a quick and easy method of retaining people's contact information.** If you don't do that, then you'll miss out on the most important benefit of attending these events.

Many times when you tell people what you do, they will want your contact info. I've often had people ask me for a business card, and I don't carry them, even though I have them. The reason why is that **I like to be in control** of whether or not I get their information… if I let my card go out into the ether, and that's it, then I might never hear from them. I'd much rather get *their* card, or… better yet… **exchange information.** When you get *their* contact info, that puts *you* in control… then you can contact them instead of waiting around for them to contact you.

I was at an event recently and exchanging info in this way, and a friend pointed me to an app called **Blinq** that brings up a QR code which you can point your phone to, and it downloads all their contact info to your phone. It worked really well. Whatever method you use… make it easy to exchange the info… and make sure you have theirs!

"Magnetize" Your Network To Make It More Effective

Earlier, in the section on Authority, we touched on "**Word Of Mouth**", which is a super-powerful force in your network. It's when people talk about you and recommend you to others, which results many times in real paying gigs… *and you didn't have to do a single thing!*

Word of Mouth is just one of the great benefits of having a robust network in place. This is where your hard work you've put into your other Client Magnet Methods really pays off… the better these are, the better your network is.

For example, when you have your **Positioning** properly in place, which we talked about earlier in Chapter 3, then that gives people a "handle" they can associate you with. If your positioning is unclear, or you do a lot of different things, then you don't give them a clear idea of what it is you do… and so they can't recommend you as strongly.

When you put your body of work in place, and it lives online, you now have a clear set of links you can share with people when they ask for your reel or portfolio.

And, of course, when you increase your **Charisma** by learning how to converse with people effectively… when they see that you're someone they would enjoy working with… you've "magnetized" your network and made it that much more powerful.

Never Stop Growing Your Network

Find a daily rhythm with your networking efforts. It's not a sprint, it's a marathon - and a little bit each day does the trick.

Develop **good networking habits** without becoming obsessive about spending too much time online. Like many people, I find that I easily get distracted with social media, so I like to make it a point to "dive in and dive out" for a set amount of time. If you make that the goal, have a set purpose and a set amount of time you intend to spend, it's easier to accomplish what you need to do without wasting a lot of time.

Let's review what we talked about in this section on growing and using our Network to magnetize our creative business.

First, we discussed how your network can grow your freelancing by **tirelessly toiling in the background**, working to get you work. The more robust your network, the more success you'll receive in more clients, more jobs, and more income.

Knowing who's who in your market and reconnecting with your past clients, keeping those contacts "warm", is essential. We also talked about some other things you can do to grow your network, such as **referring other freelancers** and **attending networking events**. The magic of **Word Of Mouth** as an authority builder is a powerful tool that cements your network and energizes it to work for you.

Before you know it, you'll be enjoying the fruits of your labor: an **interconnected hive of people that benefits you** as much as you benefit them. It's good for business… and it's good for you, too!

READY... SET... MAGNETIZE!

In this book we've discussed the **seven powerful ways** in which you can make yourself **irresistible** to your clients.

We've talked about becoming **COMPETENT** in your creative freelance field – how to know your competence level, how to increase it, and how competence yields confidence, which draws your clients in because they see that you have the confidence **and** the ability to get the job done.

Next we discussed the **AUTHORITY** factors that cement you as a go-to expert in your field… these factors convey your level of competence and make you attractive to clients as they see proof that you can do the job, making them feel comfortable in hiring you.

Then we talked about how **POSITIONING** yourself in your field of expertise makes you more magnetic because of your ability to stand out and offer your creative service in a specific, definable niche in your industry.

We talked about the different **PLATFORMS** and how they can help grow your business by making you visible to your clients and allow you a way to regularly interact with them, apply for jobs, and show your work.

I showed you how being available to your clients with the right **TIMING** makes you more attractive to them. Rather than relying on luck to make this happen, you **develop a system** for regularly and purposefully interacting with them so that you're more likely to be there when they need your services.

Next you learned about the importance of **CHARISMA** and how to develop it to improve your client interactions, grow your business, and even improve your quality of life.

Lastly, we discussed the power of your **NETWORK** of leads, clients, and peers and how all the other magnetic elements contribute to it. As you grow it, it works behind the scenes to give you clients and foster more connections.

The Client Trap

If you've ever been in the gravity well of the Disney empire (and who hasn't?) then you may be aware of a little movie called *The Parent Trap.*

The more recent one is a remake of a much older one (and yet the remake itself is old enough to feature a youthful Lindsay Lohan before some… aah… questionable life decisions…)

Anyway, my point is, not all traps are necessarily bad. And like the *Parent Trap*, which is equal parts cheesy and heartwarming, the kind of trap I'm going to talk about – **the Client Trap** – isn't a negative thing, but a huge positive win for both parties involved – you *and* your client.

Your **Client Trap** is the "icing on the cake"of the Client Magnet Method because it ensures that all the hard work we've done to attract clients actually "sticks"… maximizing our efforts by making sure aren't just *attracting* our shiny new clients, but we're also *keeping* them.

The great thing is, if you've followed and implemented any of the things I've talked about so far in this book, then you're already well on your way to devising your very own Client Trap.

Not only do you want to be magnetic to your clients, you also want to ***stay*** magnetic to them. Being "sticky" in this way ensures that you will stay in their memory banks, and that you will be near the top of their list the next time they have a job that you're well suited for.

Here are some things to weave into the fabric into your freelance business that make you "sticky"and increase your chances of getting that repeat business from these great clients.

How To Maintain Your Client Trap

- **Continue To Level Up Your Skills.**

Whenever you learn a new skill, accomplish a project, or level up your capabilities as a superstar freelancer, **share it** on social media. So that you don't seem too braggy, stay humble and positive in your speech, being extremely **complimentary of the team and clients you worked with.** Continue to update your online profiles and website with your new projects, assuming you have permission to do so. Not only will you stay visible to your clients, you'll also be showing them that you're actively engaged in furthering your skills and your business… and your authority will continue to grow in their minds.

- **Embrace Your Humanity And Uniqueness.**

In this age of A.I. and robots, **going all out on what makes you human** is the right choice. Don't be afraid to drop little personal hints that you're a real human being just like your clients. For example, be sure you have an actual picture of you on your online profile. Show up a few minutes early to online meetings, that special time when casual conversation happens, and be a part of it. Turn your camera on and make sure your snoozing pooch is visible behind you. Wear that ugly Christmas sweater or sip out of that mug that says "I have Bieber Fever", whatever makes you "you". I guarantee you'll be memorable and stick in the minds of your clients!

- **Keep Your Network Warm.**

Stay connected with your network of fellow freelancers and other creative professionals in your space. If you haven't noticed already, you may be surprised at what a **small world**

your corner of your creative market is. You never know what may come up in casual conversations, and this is important data about potential clients and work. You also never know when positive energy will flow back to your clients about *you*, further cementing your name in their minds as an authority in your space.

- **Fix The Gaps In Your "Web".**

We've talked a lot about Authority Factors like your website, online profiles, and things like that. Be sure it's **easy for your clients to get in touch with you** if they need to, and that **you are able to respond quickly** when they do. This often involves the "techy" side of things, like making sure their emails are getting delivered to you, that you have notifications turned on and that you're whitelisting your clients, and that your outgoing phone message is working. These things are easy to overlook sometimes, but they're often critical – especially those times when a client has an urgent need and they need an answer quickly.

A Few Final Words Of Encouragement

Wow! That's a lot. I know it seems like creating a business can be overwhelming, and we covered a lot of ground in this book. And we really just focused on getting clients! There's a lot of other stuff about running a creative freelance business that I teach, so if you're interested in knowing more, head on over to my blog at **creativefree lancerevolution.com/blog.** I cover a broad range of topics, from mindset to finances.

As I mentioned in the beginning of this book, I focused on getting clients because not only is it the **number one problem** freelancers have, but when you have a few great, well-paying clients, that seems to "magically" make the rest of building a freelance business lots ***easier***.

So if you are feeling overwhelmed with all the work that's ahead of you, let me take a few moments and offer some final words of encouragement.

Find The "Next Thing"... And Focus On That *Only*.

A principle that helps me is to find the s**ingle best thing** that I can work on next to further my business, and focus just on that for a while.

In fact, when we're overwhelmed, that's a sign that we're trying to take on too much at once. While many people seem to be able focus handily on more than one thing at a time, many of us (myself included) **do best with just one thing on their plate**. When you have that one thing done as much as you can for now, then shift to the next.

The key word here is "***focus***"... and **focus is incredibly powerful.** There's a simple saying that goes something like, "*Where focus goes, success follows.*" Focus also allows you go get into that magical "flow state" that allows you to lose track of time and enjoy what you're doing.

Incorporate this concept into your daily life, and you'll not only notice challenges falling away in record time, but you'll also enjoy it more, too!

Prioritize *Progress* Over Perfection.

Confession time: not only am I a recovering procrastinator, but I'm also a recovering **perfectionist**. (Really, the two are often related.) I used to get so "lost in the weeds" with a particular thing that I would not move on until I got the thing I was working on perfected to whatever nebulous standard I had in my mind.

But here's the thing: **perfect never truly arrives.**

I think we all realize this, too, deep down. What perfectionism really amounts to is this: ***fear***. Fear of moving on to the next stage, or fear of success... in any case, face whatever fear head-on that is causing you waste time perfecting the thing and causing you to delay moving forward.

On the other hand, "imperfect progress" fits very well with the "next thing" principle that we talked about previously... rather than perfecting the next step, you get it done ***good enough for now.*** And then you move on to the next thing.

How do you know how much is "good enough"? When progress starts to level off, and you feel like things aren't moving forward as drastically as they are when you first started the task. Get it to a stopping point and move on. **You can always return back to it later**, and when you do, you will probably find that along the way you've acquired some new fresh perspective, a new skill or bit of knowledge to push that task even further this time.

One more little tip on this from personal experience: when you come to a stopping point and show your client, go ahead and tell them that there is still some stuff to do, but that you wanted to get it in front of them and get their feedback. They can either say it's good enough for them, OR they might want you to go ahead and push for that final "ten percent" and make it even better. In any case, **you're making them part of the process** and including them in the decision of when it's really finished, which they will *always* appreciate.

Success Is Inevitable.

One of my coaches and mentors gave me this little wisdom nugget, and it's a great one. It comes with a caveat: **success is inevitable...** ***when we show up and do the work.***

It encourages us to get out of "the weeds" of our current problem and **zoom out our perspective** a bit. This enables us to see more clearly that if we just continue on the path, we will eventually get where we're going. The attention spans that we humans have seem to get shorter and shorter – which often works against us, causing us to shift our focus too much, fragmenting our day (and our brains!)

The "Success Is Inevitable" mantra helps us to tame the self-doubt that comes with those ADD-like habits and ensures that we not only stay focused on the task at hand, but that we also can have confidence in the end result.

Keep Your Vision Board Handy.

Another thing that helps us when we're "lost in the weeds" and feeling uncertain or overwhelmed is to go back to our Vision Board, revisit our goals, and **reconnect with our "why".**

These are powerful things that **motivate** us to keep going, and to stay the course. For example, if you feel uncertain about reaching out to a client, look at your goal of saving up enough to take your family on that trip you've always wanted to go on. Staying connected with these things can help you get over that lack of confidence you're experiencing in the moment.

Embrace Your Value As A Creative Professional.

Revisit your Unique Selling Proposition, which sets you apart from other freelancers and **cements your value** to your clients. Look at your body of work, at your positive reviews, at the past times clients have hired you to do great work and are happy they did so. **You have value!**

This isn't just vacuous pep talk. This is a real, provable fact, because you actually have hard data to back it up: a record of work that you've completed successfully as well as past clients who have paid you to do it.

Have you ever considered this? **You have even more value *now* than you did when you last worked with a particular client.** You've built a bigger portfolio, acquired even more skills, and have become a better artist. You deserve to be well compensated for what you do. ***Yes... you're worth it!***

You've Learned How To Attract Clients. Now... Go Get 'Em!

As the G.I. Joe cartoons from my Gen-X childhood once taught me, *"learning is half the battle"*. It isn't enough to merely read about this method. To reap the benefits, you have to get out there and **put it into action**.

Consider what you do in your creative field of choice... you can do it blindfolded with one hand tied behind your back. You've reached that level of "unconscious competence" that we talked about in the Four Stages Of Competence way back in Chapter 1. **But you weren't *always* good at your creative service, were you?** When you first learned your primary creative skill, you practiced, you struggled, you stuck it out... until **eventually** you achieved a **level of mastery.**

That's what I'm asking you to do here... to take these steps until eventually you reach the level of unconscious competence in the **discipline of attracting clients.** To build the different parts of this system so that you will able to have a "**Client Attraction Machine**" that works for you tirelessly to win you amazing clients, so that you win amazing jobs, and so that you can be richly rewarded with an amazing life.

It's possible. When you take the steps, it's *probable*. I know you can do it. I believe in you.

Remember the phrase "success is inevitable." It's true when you work the process, and **don't give up.**

I can't wait to hear from you... to hear how this book has helped you, to listen to how your life is forever changed because of your ability to attract clients and grow your freelance business into exactly what you want it to be.

I'd love to be part of your Network. Drop me a line at *mike@creativefreelancerevolution.com* and let me know how this book – and the principles of the Client Magnet Method – have worked for you.

See you on the other side.

Your friend and fellow freelancer,

-Mike

HERE'S HOW TO ACCESS YOUR BOOK BONUSES

If you skipped right to this part (and hey, I can't blame you!) then you probably missed the callouts within the book where to find your special bonuses that I made just for you.

You can access them here:

TheClientMagnetMethod.com

Enjoy!

ABOUT THE AUTHOR

Mike Glen Roy has been making a living from his creative pursuits for more than 20 years. He has credits in award-winning feature films and commercials as a visual effects artist and creative director. After leaving *ReelFX*, a creative studio he helped grow since 1999, he built a successful freelance business.

He's created commercial projects for a variety of national brands including Sony, Samsung, American Express, Verizon, Nestle, Gatorade, Hasbro, Coke, Pepsi, Anheuser-Busch, Lionsgate, Nike, Universal, Disney, Showtime, Dreamworks, JCPenney, Electronic Arts, Home Depot, McDonald's, Chrysler, Chevy, Ford, Toyota, Fiat, Gap, Jeep, AT&T, and Hyundai.

In addition to working on commercials, he's also worked on a number of entertainment projects such as music videos, feature films, and ride films, including *Minion Mayhem, Skull Island: Reign Of King Kong,* and *The Simpsons Ride* at Universal Studios.

After dialing in his freelance business to generate tremendous results for him and his family, he decided to become certified as a business coach and built *Creative Freelance Revolution*, a platform to coach and teach other creative freelancers to help them generate incredible results in their own lives and businesses.

Do you have any comments about this book? Or have a question about your freelance business? Connect with him at mike@creativefreelancerevolution.com, or drop him a line here: x.com/MikeGlenRoy. He can't wait to hear from ya!

Made in the USA
Monee, IL
04 November 2026

67391544R00134